E. B. WHITE

E.B. WHITE

The Elements of a Writer

by Janice Tingum

3303000013329R

LERNER PUBLICATIONS COMPANY • MINNEAPOLIS

To Kirk

The author would like to thank the following people and organizations: Joel White, Nancy Stableford, and Roger Angell for answering my questions and making available many of the materials necessary to research this book; Lucy Burgess and the staff at the Department of Rare and Manuscript Collections, Cornell University Library at Ithaca, New York, for their careful preservation of the E. B. White Collection and for providing materials and photographs; Kirk Tingum for his love, support, and advice; the Red River Children's Writers Group for their encouragement; and Susan Breckner Rose, my editor.

Library of Congress Cataloging-in-Publication Data

Tingum, Janice.
  E. B. White : the elements of a writer / Janice Tingum.
    p.   cm.
  Includes bibliographical references and index.
  ISBN 0-8225-4922-0
  1. White, E. B. (Elwyn Brooks), 1899–1985—Juvenile literature.
2. Authors, American—20th century—Biography—Juvenile
literature. 3. Children's stories—Authorship—Juvenile literature.
[1. White, E. B. (Elwyn Brooks), 1899–1985. 2. Authors, American.]
I. Title.
PS3545.H5187Z93 1995
818'.5209—dc20   94-43854
[B]   CIP
                                      AC

Manufactured in the United States of America
1 2 3 4 5 6 – JR – 00 99 98 97 96 95

Contents

Elwyn and two of his sisters round up the chickens in a barnyard.

✹ ONE ✹

101 Summit Avenue

1899–1910

Elwyn ran to the stable the moment he heard that the eggs were hatching. Fifty eggs, to be exact. He could hear the tiny beaks pecking against eggshells as he approached the warming tray.

The small, thin boy strained to see over the table. One by one, the chicks emerged. Elwyn squirmed with delight as the wet little birds pushed their broken shells away.

When the pecking finally stopped, all the eggs had hatched, except three. The family's coachman declared the three eggs worthless and disposed of them, unbroken, in a manure pile outside. Elwyn lingered near the new chicks, observing their first halting steps. He was amazed at the miracle of an egg.

After a while, Elwyn heard a distant peeping sound. Running outside to investigate, he found three newly hatched chicks in the manure pile. They were quickly rescued and returned to the stable.

Many years later, in 1952, Elwyn wrote *Charlotte's Web,* a very popular book about a pig named Wilbur whose friend rescues him from death. By then, Elwyn, professionally known as E. B. White, was already an accomplished writer of essays and editorials for *The New Yorker* and *Harper's Magazine*. In his lifetime, Elwyn wrote three best-selling children's books. In them, he shared his love for the barn, his respect for nature, and his awe at the miracle of an egg.

Elwyn Brooks White was born on July 11, 1899, in Mount Vernon, New York. The peaceful Manhattan suburb suited the Whites' quiet, affluent lifestyle. To Elwyn, his home at 101 Summit Avenue—with its huge front door, tall pillars, and octagonal tower—was like a fortress. From the second-story

Elwyn grew up at 101 Summit Avenue, a fortress of a house with a stable in the back.

porches, a boy could defend against any intruder who dared to pass the neatly trimmed hedges bordering the lot.

Elwyn often retreated to the stable behind the house. There he tended an assortment of birds, reptiles, and rodents. The stable smelled of hay, axle grease, and manure. Elwyn liked this place, which was as near to a barn as he could get.

In the winter, he met friends at a pond for skating and ice hockey. When they tired of skating, the boys coasted down a small hill near the White home. Sometimes they persuaded a neighbor to let them swing from a barn loft rope.

Elwyn's father, Samuel Tilly White, commuted by train to his job in New York City. He worked for the piano firm of Horace Waters & Company. By the time Elwyn was born,

The White family, left to right: *Lillian, Samuel, Albert, Jessie, Elwyn, Stanley, Marion, and Clara*

Clara White holds her baby brother, Elwyn.

Mr. White was vice-president and secretary of the company. He later became its president.

The piano firm prospered even when conditions in the city worsened. In New York City, thousands of people lived in crowded, run-down tenements. A financial crisis, the Panic of 1907, caused many businesses to become bankrupt. Unemployed workers stood in long soup lines for food. The White family, however, seemed unaffected by these events.

Elwyn liked to experiment with the many musical instruments his father brought home from work. He tried out the grand piano, drums, and guitars. He took music lessons and even tried to compose songs, but Elwyn never considered himself a talented musician.

Elwyn's mother, Jessie Hart White, was the daughter of the well-known painter, William Hart. A hardworking and affectionate person, Mrs. White preferred to spend time at home with her family rather than entertain guests or attend social events. She employed several servants to help with the children and household chores.

As the Whites' youngest child, Elwyn was surrounded by grown-ups. By the time he was in kindergarten, his sisters Marion and Clara were married. A few years later, his brothers, Albert and Stanley, left for Cornell University. Lillian—five years older than Elwyn—was closest in age. Mr. and Mrs. White also had a daughter, Janet, who died in infancy.

When the first day of kindergarten arrived, Elwyn screamed and had a temper tantrum. He did not want to go.

Five-year-old Elwyn loved to spend time around animals.

But Mr. and Mrs. White were equally determined and finally succeeded in getting their son to school. To Elwyn's dismay, a girl in his class kept trying to hold his hand.

In addition to the trauma of going to school, Elwyn experienced itchy eyes and an annoying runny nose. The condition worsened on Sunday afternoons when he rode in the surrey. Elwyn told his father that the smell of the horse bothered him. Mr. White called a doctor to the house, who reported that Elwyn had "catarrhal trouble."

"Douse his head in cold water every morning before breakfast," the doctor told Mrs. White. So for two years, Elwyn endured the routine of an early-morning cold water spray. His allergies, however, troubled him for the rest of his life.

By the time he entered first grade, Elwyn knew how to read. Stanley taught his little brother to sound out the words printed in their father's newspaper, the *New York Times*. Elwyn loved to match rhyming words and make up poems. After that, he quickly learned how to write. "This is where I belong," he thought about writing. "This is it."

Elwyn began keeping a journal when he was about eight years old. He also wrote poems and short stories, mostly about animals. One day he submitted a poem to a writing contest in a women's magazine. It was a sad tale about a mouse who cautiously stepped into a trap to get a piece of cheese. The trap sprung and killed the mouse. The young poet advised that "mice had better be careful, and not try to be too wise." For his entry, Elwyn won a book.

One day he received a crate in the mail from his sister Clara in Washington, D.C. Inside, he found a collie puppy, which he promptly named Mac. Elwyn wanted to keep the dog in the house, but his parents objected because they wanted to keep the house clean. The stable was too cold. Mac had to

Elwyn poses
with his brothers,
Albert (center)
and Stanley
(right), *in 1906.*

sleep in the basement where the coal was stored. Elwyn felt
bad that Mac had such poor quarters, so he built a special stall
in the stable, lined with sheepskin to help keep the dog warm.

Elwyn earned good grades in school, but he dreaded the
student assembly. Each day a student was called on to recite
a piece in front of all the other students. This terrified Elwyn.
The students were selected in alphabetical order according to
their last names. Often, the letter *W* was never reached by
the end of the school term, and Elwyn did not have to recite.
Still, the possibility of speaking in front of the student assembly
was one of the things that troubled him.

Elwyn was fearful of many things. He was nervous about
the start of school each year. He was afraid of going down to
the boys' bathroom in the school basement. And he was over-
ly concerned that he might embarrass himself in front of others.

Elwyn enjoys the peacefulness of summer vacation at the Belgrade Lakes in Maine.

 TWO

New Experiences

1910–1917

While the school term seemed to burden Elwyn with its social demands, summer vacation was filled with fun. August was the best month. It was then that the White family traveled to the Belgrade Lakes in Maine for their annual vacation. Mr. White enjoyed the outdoors and thought the crisp Maine air might relieve Elwyn's allergies. For Elwyn it was an adventure.

Preparation for the trip involved weeks of packing clothes, purchasing train tickets, and notifying friends. The journey began with a commuter train ride from Mount Vernon into New York City. After a meal in Grand Central Station, Elwyn and his family boarded the evening Bar Harbor Express.

The express, a train with many compartments and Pullman-car berths, chugged along through the night. Drawing a thin, brown blanket to his chin, Elwyn tried to sleep.

At nine o'clock the next morning, the express pulled into the Belgrade railway station. A local farmer loaded their luggage onto a horse-drawn wagon and drove them the final 10 miles to a cabin on Great Pond.

Members of the White family make an excursion in a rowboat named Jessie *across the lake to Bean's general store.*

When the Whites arrived at the lakefront, Stanley and Albert would launch their homemade boat, *Jessie*. Mrs. White, for whom the boat was named, hated the water. Nonetheless, she nervously boarded the little vessel for a family excursion around the lake. With Albert and Stanley minding the engine, they navigated their way through Belgrade Stream to Bean's general store. While the children fed fish from the wharf, Mr. White bought Moxie or birch beer for the family. Despite his concerns that the boat was too crowded, Elwyn loved the water and the thrill of this family outing.

During the time in Maine, Elwyn would sneak out to the lake in the early morning while the rest of the family slept. It was so peaceful here, with the tall birch trees behind him and the calm water before him. Just as he enjoyed the sounds and smells of the stable at home, Elwyn felt a contentment here in the company of frogs, fish, and birds along the lake.

When Elwyn was 11 years old, he was delighted to receive a 16-foot Old Town canoe from his father. It was dark green with the name ELWYN printed in large white letters on the bow. Stanley taught his little brother how to paddle so that the canoe ran a straight course. Stanley also showed Elwyn how to use a jackknife and explained scientific laws, such as centrifugal force, gravity, and inertia.

Stanley canoes on the calm water of the Belgrade Lakes.

Elwyn made this pamphlet for a friend from home.

The summer vacation passed quickly, and Elwyn dreaded returning to school. He also worried about the future. As he watched his older siblings attend college, find jobs, and get married, Elwyn began to fret about these things too, even though it would be many years before he would face those events. He was also worried about his health and the meaning of life and death. Writing helped pass the time and ease his mind.

St. Nicholas magazine invited children to submit poems, stories, pictures, and puzzles. Winning entries were published, and the authors received a gold or silver badge. Elwyn yearned to win a badge and see his writing published. A friend pointed out that most of the winning entries dealt with the kind treatment of animals. So Elwyn wrote a story about a dog named Don and a walk through the woods in winter. In the story, Don wanted to chase after squirrels, rabbits, and quail, but Elwyn made sure no harm came to the small animals. One of his parents wrote "This is Elwyn's own work" on the back of the manuscript. With a mixture of excitement and hope, he mailed the story to *St. Nicholas.*

Elwyn won the silver badge for "A Winter Walk," which appeared in the June 1911 issue of the magazine. Even though his first name was misspelled as "Elwin," his joy in being published was not diminished. He was a writer.

Almost every month, for three or four years, Elwyn sent manuscripts to the *St. Nicholas* magazine. His writing improved, and he won honorable mention several times. In 1914 he submitted another dog story, this one about the family's Irish setter. For "A True Dog Story," he won the coveted gold badge.

Elwyn entered Mount Vernon High School in the fall of 1913. The following summer, the First World War erupted in Europe. Many Americans argued for neutrality, saying that the United States should not become involved in the troubles abroad. Elwyn, however, did not pay much attention to the war. Instead, he focused on the everyday worries of high school. He was awkward in sports, but he liked Latin class and biology, where he drew pictures of beans and frogs. In his free time, Elwyn continued to tend his animals in the stable.

Even though he was allergic to horses, Elwyn loved them.

Samuel White with his son Elwyn in 1914

Elwyn liked Eileen Thomas, who lived on the same street as the Whites. He imagined taking Eileen to a school dance or out for a soda. But every time he walked past her house, Elwyn tensed with nervousness.

Lillian, a popular redhead, attempted to teach her 16-year-old brother to dance, but he was still very awkward. One day, they went to the Plaza Hotel in New York and watched couples on the dance floor swinging to the music. Elwyn decided to take Eileen there, where the sophistication and beauty of the Plaza Hotel could hide his nervousness.

For three days, he planned his date—counting his money, selecting clothes, checking train schedules, and practicing his phone call to Eileen. One evening when his parents were out of earshot, Elwyn telephoned Eileen and arranged the date.

At the designated time, the two met and walked to the

train depot. Train and bus connections occurred as planned, but the conversation was strained. At the Plaza, Elwyn and Eileen dutifully ate cinnamon toast and danced. The emotional strain of the evening was too much for Elwyn, however. Eager to end the date, he decided against having dinner in the city and took Eileen home.

In the summer of 1916, Elwyn skipped the annual trip to the Belgrade Lakes in favor of some independence and took a job as a golf caddy at the Lake Placid Club. When winter arrived, he spent his free time skating with friends on Siwanoy Pond at the edge of Mount Vernon. Often the boys and girls skated in pairs. Although he feared dancing, Elwyn felt at ease skating with a girl.

Mildred Hesse, a popular classmate with pretty blue eyes, caught Elwyn's attention. He waited for his turn to skate with her. When he had his chance, Elwyn offered Mildred the end of a piece of bicycle tape. Together they skated, each gripping the end of the tape.

Eventually the bicycle tape disappeared, and they circled the pond, hand in hand, "gliding into the woods on narrow fingers of ice." After an evening at the pond, Elwyn returned home and played romantic songs on the piano. He was in love. Mildred, however, was probably unaware of Elwyn's feelings, since he confided only in his journal.

By the time he was a junior at Mount Vernon High School, Elwyn had gone from writing simple dog stories to writing on political and social issues. In the spring of 1916, he submitted a short story entitled "Pink Hats" to the high school newspaper. The story revealed Elwyn's preoccupation with adult matters. The main characters were a newly married couple dealing with the issue of jealousy. With an eye for detail, he wrote: "The cause of this highly unfortunate quarrel was nothing more or less than a rather diminutive pink straw hat with racing lines and a stiff white feather growing from the stern at a devilish angle."

Later, as an assistant editor of the *Oracle,* the school magazine, Elwyn wrote an editorial arguing that the country should stay out of the war in Europe. The editorial reflected a genuine interest in political affairs, and even more so, it showed his developing writing style. In just five paragraphs, Elwyn made several literary references to the Bible and to Greek mythology, relied upon an anecdote to illustrate a point, and used metaphors to enlighten the reader. "It's an art to know how to stay out," he wrote, "and it has to be cultivated just the same as potatoes do."

President Wilson's efforts to keep the country neutral failed. On February 3, 1917, a German submarine sank an American ship, and the United States severed diplomatic relations with Germany. On April 6, 1917, the United States Congress declared war on Germany.

At this point, Elwyn became a staunch supporter of the nation's efforts. "Personal views must not affect individual action," Elwyn wrote in a 1917 editorial. "Our duty is the same, whatever our opinion may be!"

After graduating from high school, Elwyn struggled with his obligation to his country. He wrote in his journal, "So much history is being made every minute that it's up to every last one of us to see that it's the right kind of history."

But Elwyn did not know how to help. He was too small to join the army and unqualified to fly airplanes. He considered joining the American Ambulance Corps in France, but his mother opposed the idea. Finally, to assuage his guilt, Elwyn took a summer job in the military, working as a cadet on a Long Island farm.

As a student at Cornell University, Elwyn acquired the nickname "Andy." This formal portrait was taken in 1920.

❧ THREE ❧

Ithaca, New York

1917–1921

From the time Stanley and Albert were students at Cornell University, Elwyn planned to follow in his brothers' footsteps. So in September 1917, Elwyn, a slender young man with wavy hair and twinkling gray eyes, arrived in Ithaca to enter Cornell.

Several days before school began, he joined others in line waiting to get an application form for a scholarship test. When he reached the front of the line, he mistakenly picked up the wrong form. The registrar yelled at Elwyn and called him a thief. Elwyn froze in fear. He returned to his room, lay down on the bed, and cried. Embarrassed and angry, he decided to leave Cornell.

But a few hours later, after he had calmed down, he wrote an apology to the registrar. Elwyn took the test and won a scholarship. His scholarship totaled one thousand dollars, which was more than sufficient to meet tuition costs.

With college enrollment still a few days off, Elwyn set out to explore Ithaca. He was having so much fun in town that he

A view of Boardman Hall and the clock tower on the Cornell University campus in 1921

carelessly missed the freshmen registration. By the time he did enroll, classes had already begun.

Elwyn's apathy for school did not improve, and his schoolwork suffered. Homesick, he took long, lonely walks. He was ill for a week and imagined the worst—consumption, or tuberculosis.

The Phi Gamma Delta fraternity invited Elwyn to join its membership, but he was not sure he would fit in with the other students. Although he was in college now, Elwyn was still insecure in social settings. "Have confidence in yourself," his sister Lillian urged. Elwyn took her advice and joined the fraternity.

At Cornell the students called Elwyn "Andy." The first president of the college was Andrew White, and the students affectionately called any male student with the White surname "Andy." Elwyn liked this new name.

"Andy" enjoyed writing articles for the *Cornell Daily Sun*. The college newspaper came out six mornings a week, carrying both local and national news. Each year, the freshman writers competed for a position on the *Sun* board, the winner having published the most column inches during the year. Andy came in second in the number of column inches, but because he was well-respected for his reporting ability, insightful comments, and witty headlines, he was awarded the board position anyway.

Journalism professor Bristow Adams invited Andy to his home, where Mrs. Adams served cocoa and the two men talked. Sometimes Andy stopped by to chat or play the piano. On Monday evenings, Professor Adams entertained a group of journalism students. Their conversation ranged from newspaper ethics to international events. These stimulating discussions caused Andy to think for himself, forcing him to form his own opinions on serious issues.

Perhaps the biggest discovery for Andy came through his history class. As the professor lectured about the oppression that existed during the Middle Ages, Andy suddenly realized the importance of a free society. No longer could he take his own freedom for granted.

While Andy's opinions were tested in the Adams's home, his writing was scrutinized at the Manuscript Club, which met monthly at the home of Professor Martin Sampson. Here, professors and students critiqued each other's poems and stories. Andy enjoyed both the friendship and intellectual stimulation of the meetings. In a *Sun* editorial, he argued that more

Martin W. Sampson, above, and William Strunk, right, were two of Andy's professors.

learning occurred in such informal discussions between students and professors than in a controlled 50-minute class period.

One of the professors who attended the Manuscript Club was William Strunk, author of *The Elements of Style,* a practical guide to English usage. Andy later took Strunk's English VIII class and learned important rules for writing. "Omit needless words," Professor Strunk ordered his students.

One of Andy's closest friends at Cornell was fellow writer Howard "Cush" Cushman. The two both attended the Manuscript Club and contributed articles to the *Sun.* Andy and Cush sometimes talked about taking a car trip across the United States, just for fun.

On September 12, 1918, Andy registered for the draft. He entered his sophomore year at Cornell, determined to improve his grades and serve his country. He immediately enlisted in the Student Army Training Corps. Within a month he was promoted to corporal. His classes included military law, war aims, and drill.

On November 11, 1918, Andy awakened to the sound of bells. Chimes rang out the national anthem. "The war is over!" the students yelled. The next day Andy wrote in his journal, "Yesterday was one of the greatest days in the history of the world."

In his junior year, Andy began dating Alice Burchfield, a petite, outgoing chemistry major from Buffalo, New York. Andy took Alice to sporting events and movies. They watched for falling stars together. And Andy wrote love poems, which he arranged to get published in the *Sun* using a pseudonym. The stilted conversation and awkwardness of his high school date with Eileen Thomas were gone.

In addition to serving on the *Sun*'s board of editors, Andy was chosen editor-in-chief of the paper and elected president of his fraternity. Frequently his editorials dealt with the issue of free speech. "Some thoughts may be uttered freely, and others are a bit free when uttered," he wrote in 1920. He went on to distinguish between the right of free speech and the "right to use bad judgment," which often interferes with free speech. Another time he criticized students for being sloppy in their speech and lacking ability to communicate well-thought-out opinions. Clearly, Andy took his role as a writer and editor seriously.

By the time he graduated in 1921, he had published over

A newspaper clipping announces E. B. White's position as editor-in-chief of the Cornell Sun.

180 editorials, addressing issues such as fraternity membership requirements, Communist teachers, and racial prejudice. One of his editorials on free speech won first prize in a competition at the Convention of Eastern College Newspapers.

Following graduation, Andy worked for a summer as a counselor with Cush and another friend, Robert Hubbard, at a boys' camp near Dorset, Ontario. Unlike the Belgrade Lakes, Camp Otter was a wooded wilderness with overgrown trails.

One evening, a boy fell ill during a hike 11 miles from the camp. Andy and Robert set out at sunset to take the boy to a doctor. They canoed across four lakes. On the portages between lakes, Robert carried the boy and Andy carried the canoe. Muddy, hungry, and tired, they hiked the final two miles to camp in total darkness. The boy was promptly treated.

Alice Burchfield and Andy dated each other during college.

Andy and Robert devoured a package of cookies that Alice had sent.

After camp closed, Andy spent a few days looking for work in Ithaca in hopes of remaining near Alice. His search was futile, however. On his last evening there, Andy and Alice strolled through Percy Field. By this time, their relationship had deepened into love, and Andy thought about proposing marriage to Alice. But not being sure of himself, he hesitated and did not mention it. As they parted, Andy promised to write as soon as he found work.

Professor Sampson offered to help Andy find a job teaching at a university. Because of his fear of public speaking, Andy declined the offer. Instead, he hoped to pursue his interest in writing.

Andy's Model T, Hotspur, *holds up one end of a tent.*

FOUR

Hotspur

1921–1925

In the fall of 1921, Andy returned to his parents' home in Mount Vernon and took the train to New York City to look for a job. On his first day, Andy interviewed with the managing editor of the *Post* and the city editor of the *Sun*. Both editors said they were overstaffed.

Andy was not discouraged. After six days, he had two job offers. New York Edison Company asked him to edit their in-house paper; United Press offered him a job feeding news wire. The Edison Company position included a plush private office and a personal stenographer. But Andy accepted the job with United Press because it was fast-paced, demanding, and dealt with current news stories.

It was Andy's job to edit the news bulletins that came in on the telegraph wires and send them out again to several newspapers. The bulletins came in very fast and by the time Andy was finished with his day's work, he was exhausted. One day he worked from eight o'clock in the morning until after nine o'clock at night, with only half an hour off for lunch.

After a few weeks on the job, Andy was asked to report

on the funeral of Senator Philander C. Knox at Valley Forge. Andy missed his train and arrived just as the casket was being lowered into the ground. This failure on his first reporting assignment proved to be too great of an embarrassment for Andy. Doubting his ability to be a reporter, he quit his job.

But Andy could not ignore his desire to write, so he applied to newspaper editors in Connecticut, Michigan, and New York. He even placed a "Position Wanted" advertisement.

A friend arranged for Andy to interview with Adolph Ochs, the publisher of the *New York Times*. Andy was very nervous about meeting such an important newspaperman, but he felt obligated to his friend to keep the appointment. Armed with a list of prepared answers for possible questions, Andy headed for the *Times* building. But as the elevator rose to Ochs's 11th-floor office, Andy's confidence fell, and he decided not to request a job from the publisher. So when Ochs asked Andy what he wanted, Andy only asked for some career advice. Ochs recommended that Andy find a job with a small-town newspaper, where he could get broad experience in all areas of journalism.

During the next few months, Andy tried several public relations jobs, but he complained that the work was painful and boring. Andy continued to correspond with Alice. Their letters were polite but not sentimental. In his spare time, Andy composed poems and stories to sell to local magazines and newspapers.

Andy was restless. For some time he had toyed with the idea of the cross-country car trip that he and Cush had discussed during college.

When Cush flunked out of Cornell in February of 1922, he looked up Andy in New York. A trip was the main topic of their conversation. Soon it was all decided. Andy would quit his job, and the two men would begin their trip. They would sell articles about their adventures to pay for trip expenses.

Several months earlier, Andy had purchased *Hotspur,* a Model T roadster. Andy felt like a king when he drove *Hotspur* with its top down and the wind blowing across his face. He was proud of his car with its new leather smell and the rumbling sound it made at about 28 miles per hour. With a few adaptations, *Hotspur* would be perfect transportation for the trip.

A blacksmith secured two iron braces to the car's left running board in order to support an army footlocker. The footlocker was packed with sweaters, notebook paper, stationery, a tripod for the typewriter, Cush's money belt, a hunting knife, a whetstone, 18 pairs of socks, 2 journal covers, some magazines, and an assortment of small items. A wooden box containing *Webster's Collegiate Dictionary* and other books was secured atop the footlocker.

A bracket was also attached to the right running board to keep a suitcase in place. In addition to clothing, the men packed

Cush, shown here in Hotspur*'s passenger's seat, could not drive.*

two Corona typewriters, a can of grease, 40 feet of rope, a jack, extra shoes, a briefcase, a bedroll, tent, blanket, and ponchos. They stowed cooking supplies in college laundry bags and hung the bags on the side of the car. A cigar-box fiddle and Cush's mouth organ were the final items on their list.

One evening before leaving, the two friends drove to Mount Vernon to inform Andy's parents of the trip. Fearing that his parents would not approve, Andy had delayed telling them of his plans. Although they did not share Andy's enthusiasm, Mr. and Mrs. White did not object to the trip.

Andy was also concerned about how Alice would react to his travel plans. During the year since Andy had graduated from Cornell, their relationship had become more distant and formal. Andy was no longer sure how Alice felt about him. But he knew he should talk to her before leaving on his trip.

After three days, Andy and Cush arrived in Ithaca. They spent five days renewing old friendships, writing for the Cornell *Sun,* playing the fiddle and mouth organ, and talking about the trip. But Andy avoided Alice. He had heard a rumor that Alice was engaged.

A snowstorm hit Ithaca on the travelers' last day there. With no more time to stall, Andy waited for Alice near a campus bridge she would cross on her way to class, but she was sick that day and did not appear.

A short time later, Andy visited Alice in her hometown of Buffalo, New York. To his surprise, he learned that Alice was not engaged. Andy, who had never even told Alice that he loved her, hesitantly asked her to marry him. Surprised, Alice declined the proposal, but the pair agreed to continue corresponding.

To a college friend Andy confided: "Cush and I are both bent on the profession of writing, and just now we are interested

On their way from New York to Seattle, Cush and Andy spent many nights tenting out next to Hotspur.

in seeing all sorts of people and all kinds of country, so that we will at least know where to begin."

With the popular touring "Blue Book" as their travel guide, Andy and Cush left New York. Most nights they slept beneath the stars in their pup tent and bedrolls. Occasionally, they roomed at a fraternity house, YMCA, or stayed with a friend of a friend.

For several weeks, they wandered through parts of Ohio, the Blue Grass region of Kentucky, and West Virginia. They crossed the Ohio River on a ferry boat and slept along a creek bed.

A horse race was on when the two men arrived in Lexington, Kentucky. Both were novices at placing bets, but decided to look into it. Cush pored over newspapers and advice sheets as he tried to pick the most logical winner. He finally settled on John F. Turner, the favored horse.

Andy, however, did not take the race seriously. After reviewing the list of mares in the race, he placed a two dollar bet on Auntie May because he liked the name. It didn't concern him that the odds were against Auntie May. To Cush's surprise, it was Auntie May who won the race, earning Andy almost 25 dollars. John F. Turner did not even place.

Andy and Cush next headed for the Kentucky Derby at Churchill Downs. This time, however, neither man was lucky. That evening, as the two men ate supper at their campsite by the city dump, Andy grabbed a napkin and wrote a poem on it in honor of the winning horse. Ignoring Cush's embarrassment, Andy drove into town, parked the car under a streetlight, and typed up the sonnet.

"Now I shall sell it," he announced.

Later that evening, the editor of the *Louisville Herald* asked Andy, "Do you do this for glory or for money?"

"I do it for money," Andy replied. The editor paid Andy five dollars. The next day the sonnet appeared under the byline "Elwyn Brooks White" on the front page of the *Herald*.

Andy and Cush continued through Indiana, Illinois, Wisconsin, and into Minneapolis, Minnesota. By this time they had only 76 cents left. To earn money, Andy helped a college student write two philosophy papers, mailed letters for an advertising agency, and sold roach powder.

The *Minneapolis Journal* sponsored a limerick contest and Andy won 25 dollars for the best entry. He also sold an article to the *Minneapolis Sunday Tribune*.

Andy fell and dislocated his right elbow in Walker, Minnesota. A doctor put a plaster cast on the elbow. The next day, Andy had his arm x-rayed at a tuberculosis sanitarium. When he learned that the bones were fine and that it was only his muscles and ligaments that ached, he had Cush cut the cast off with a hunting knife. Andy would not allow the injury to slow their trip.

At the Becker Cafe in Hardin, Montana, Andy played the piano in exchange for meals.

Andy and Cush found many ways to earn money. In Montana, Cush worked as a farmhand; Andy played piano in a café. They sanded a dance floor, washed dishes, ran a carnival concession stand, and worked on a ranch.

In Cody, Wyoming, they were low on funds, so Andy sold his typewriter for 20 dollars. Then, while in Alberta, Canada, one of *Hotspur*'s tires blew. Andy walked 32 miles into town reciting poetry and carrying Cush's typewriter. He sold the typewriter and bought a new tire for the car.

In Spokane, Washington, Andy received a letter from his father advising him to sell *Hotspur* and take a train home. Alice also wrote, enclosing five dollars, which Andy resolved not to spend. A few days later, however, he was forced to use part of Alice's money for car repairs and food.

Andy and Cush arrived in Seattle in the middle of September. In a letter to Alice, Andy confided that he was homesick but still not ready to go home. He sold *Hotspur* and purchased a new Ford coupe. After an unsuccessful job search, Cush returned home. Andy, however, landed a reporter's job at the *Seattle Times*. His pay was 40 dollars a week. Mr. Johns, the city editor, discovered that Andy's writing style was not suited to serious news events, because Andy liked to write with a humorous slant. In addition, tragedies so upset him that he was incapable of reporting on these events.

The editor asked Andy to write feature articles and a daily "Personal Column" consisting of short poems, paragraphs, humorous question/answer pieces, and anecdotes. Andy enjoyed this outlet for his creative writing.

One day, while Andy was trying to find the right words to express a thought, he asked Mr. Johns for advice.

"Just say the words," Mr. Johns said.

"I always remembered that," Andy wrote years later. "It was excellent advice and I am still trying to say the words."

After 11 months and almost 80 "Personal Columns," Andy lost his position at the *Times* due to job cutbacks. Mr. Johns told Andy that his dismissal was not a reflection on his ability. Andy was not so sure. Nonetheless, he felt relieved to be free of obligations again.

Still restless, Andy would not consider returning to New York. Alice's letters remained friendly and often contained gifts, such as a necktie or embroidered handkerchief. If she was interested in reviving their relationship, Andy did not appear to notice. His own letters were often self-centered and critical of the items Alice had sent.

Andy found work as a reporter for the Seattle Times *in 1922.*

Andy read about a steamer ship, the SS *Buford*, which was sailing to Alaska to establish business between San Francisco and Alaska, a U.S. territory. The public was invited to join the cruise. The prospect of such a trip intrigued Andy.

But the six-week trip was expensive. Andy had only 40 dollars. For several days he hung around the dock, trying to befriend the crew and secure a job. When this failed, he purchased a ticket to sail on the *Buford* as far as Skagway, Alaska. He hoped that by the time they reached Skagway, he could find a job on ship and continue the voyage.

The *Buford* departed from Seattle on July 24, 1923, under the command of Captain Louis L. Lane. The next evening, the guests buzzed with excitement. In the distance, a tall gray ship carrying President Harding lingered near the shore. As the *Buford* passed the ship, the president waved to them with a handkerchief. A short time later, President Harding died unexpectedly, and the *Buford* crew held a memorial service on board.

As a first-class passenger, Andy danced to the music of the Six Brown Brothers saxophone ensemble and dined with the other passengers. All the way to Skagway, Andy continued to ask crew members for a job.

At Skagway, Andy sat on the deck, dolefully watching the passengers file off the ship. Just then, a girl gave him a message to see the captain.

"We can put you on as night saloonsman for the remainder of the voyage—workaway passage. Is that satisfactory?" Captain Lane asked.

That evening the guests were surprised to see Andy dressed in a white waiter's coat, taking their orders, serving food, washing dishes, and shining the brass. At first Andy was embarrassed by the change in his status, but soon he saw humor in it and took secret pleasure in the guests' confused looks.

As part of the crew, Andy could not socialize with the passengers. He was even prohibited from sitting down while on deck, but Andy preferred his working status to passenger life. He liked to think of himself as a working man.

Shortly thereafter, Andy was assigned to work as a fireman's mess boy in the lowest part of the ship, among the rough men who kept the ship's engines hot. This dark steamy place smelled of garbage and dirt.

Andy nervously served the firemen their meals, carrying pots of food from the main galley down a steep ladder into the mess room. The firemen were argumentative and hard to please, but Andy won their approval with exaggerated hard-luck stories about his past. He told the men that he had been repeatedly fired from his previous jobs. The men called him "Mess."

On the return trip, a heavy gale shook the ship for three days, throwing food off of tables, breaking pipes, and making passengers and crew sick. Andy discovered that if he didn't resist the tossing of the ship, he would not get sick. With a sense of victory, he hurried about, tending the sick firemen.

On September 4, 1923, the adventure ended. The *Buford* released Andy at Seattle, and soon he was on a train, headed for New York.

Andy stopped at Buffalo to visit Alice. Their visit was very formal, revealing the strain of their long separation. They continued to correspond after Andy returned to Mount Vernon, but the letters only brought misunderstanding. Finally, in the spring of 1924, Andy wrote a letter to Alice to apologize for his "bungling ways" and to end the relationship.

For a year and a half after his return from Seattle, Andy drifted between advertising production jobs, freelance writing, unemployment, and travel. Living with his parents and working in Manhattan, he was still restless and unable to find a satisfying job.

Andy White and James Thurber

❦ FIVE ❧

The New Yorker
1925–1929

On February 21, 1925, Andy hurried to buy a new magazine on sale in Grand Central Station. The cover of this first issue featured a cartoon drawing of an elegantly dressed man examining a butterfly through a monocle.

Andy's excitement grew as he paged through *The New Yorker*. Its articles covered drama, literature, current events, and interesting people. Most of all, Andy enjoyed the magazine's satirical wit.

Harold Ross, a temperamental but determined journalist, edited *The New Yorker*. He intended the weekly magazine to be a sophisticated, tasteful, and witty cultural guide to New York City. In many ways, Ross seemed an unlikely person to start a magazine for a sophisticated audience. A high school dropout, he had jumped from one journalism job to another throughout his career. Although *The New Yorker* was targeted to fashion-conscious readers, Ross paid little attention to his own appearance. His coarse dark hair stood straight up on his

Harold Ross, editor of The New Yorker.

head. Clothing hung loose on his gangly body. Wild gestures and swear words punctuated his speech.

Ross's editorial skills and appreciation of satirical humor had been sharpened by a group of writer friends who regularly met for lunch at the Algonquin Hotel in New York City. The group, known as the Algonquin Round Table, engaged in lively literary discussions.

With articles written by members of the Round Table and with financial support from Raoul Fleischmann, a wealthy businessman, *The New Yorker* made its debut. After reading the first issue, Andy submitted several short articles. Nine weeks later, a humorous piece he had written about spring appeared in the magazine. Then, a little later, his article "Defense of the Bronx River" was printed.

Andy was thrilled by his sales to *The New Yorker*. But the magazine still struggled to succeed. In the first few months, circulation dropped. Fleischmann put more money into the project. Ross reorganized the layout and hired additional editors.

In the summer of 1925, Ross hired Katharine Angell to read manuscripts on a part-time basis. A graduate of Bryn Mawr College in Pennsylvania, she had an exceptional ability to identify quality writing. Soon she was working full-time as an editorial assistant.

Katharine brought order and stability to *The New Yorker* offices. Her calm manner and self-confidence contrasted with Ross's disheveled ways. She encouraged good writers. One of those writers signed his submissions "E. B. W."

Andy was less certain about his abilities. In the summer of 1925, he quit his job at J. H. Newmark, an advertising agency. Listless, he passed the time in Grand Central Station, at the zoo, and at the library. A few months later, he returned to his job at J. H. Newmark and moved from his parents' home into an apartment with three college friends in Greenwich Village.

One day, a waitress at Child's restaurant accidentally spilled a glass of buttermilk on Andy. Embarrassed, she scurried about cleaning off Andy's blue suit. Instead of getting angry or upset, Andy saw humor in the incident. He wrote a 650-word article about the event and submitted "Child's Play" to *The New Yorker.*

Of the waitress, Andy wrote, "In my ear she whispered a million apologies, hopelessly garbled, infinitely forlorn." The rest of the diners watched him approach the cashier. Andy wrote, "I could almost hear the unvoiced question rising from a hundred throats: 'Surely he isn't going to *pay the check*?'" Not only did he pay the bill and leave a tip, but when the cashier handed him his change, "I waved it splendidly aside." Andy wrote, "'Let that take care of the buttermilk.'"

Readers liked the article and Andy experienced "a sudden burst of confidence and of wellbeing." He realized that he could communicate with readers and earn money, simply by writing about himself, even about his misfortunes.

One evening in 1926, Andy fell asleep on a train while returning to New York. He dreamed about a mouselike boy who wore a hat and walked briskly with a cane. When he awoke, Andy wrote a few notes about the dream.

The character came in handy when Andy's nephews and nieces begged for a story. Andy was not very good at making up impromptu tales. He needed to write them down first. So Andy named the mouselike boy Stuart and wrote short adventures about him, which he shared with the children.

At *The New Yorker*, Katharine recognized a special quality in Andy's writing. At her urging, Harold Ross invited Andy to stop by the magazine's office. Andy didn't respond to Ross's invitation right away, but one day he stopped by the office. Katharine greeted him.

"Are you Elwyn Brooks White?" she asked. Katharine's gentle manner put Andy at ease. She listened attentively, answered his questions, and praised his writing. Soon after, Andy agreed to edit newsbreaks for *The New Yorker.*

Newsbreaks were very short items found in other publications, which were funny because they contained a grammatical error or awkward phrasing. Andy added a brief, witty punch line of his own to each item. For example, a local paper reported: "Besides selecting Mrs. Ross and Mrs. Farley as vice-chairmen to work with him in the campaign, Raskob also kicked Mayor Frank Hague of Jersey City."

To this quote, Andy added the punch line: "And called it a day."

Andy also developed newsbreak departments, such as "Neatest Trick of the Week," which contained items such as this sentence from the *Herald Tribune:* "The outstanding exhibit of the show was the group of chrysanthemums covering 150 square feet of Mr. J. P. Morgan."

Ross liked Andy's work and asked him to join *The New Yorker*'s staff. Andy hesitated. Ross and Katharine persisted, sometimes inviting Andy out for lunch to discuss it further. But Andy would not commit himself to *The New Yorker.* Instead, he took a trip to Europe with a friend who was making an advertising film.

Andy and Ross finally reached an agreement in January 1927. Andy agreed to split his time between *The New Yorker* and J. H. Newmark. Each employer paid him 30 dollars a week. Eventually, Andy left J. H. Newmark in order to devote more time to *The New Yorker.* Wary of commitment, however, he refused to accept regular office hours.

Andy found his niche at *The New Yorker* in the column entitled "Talk of the Town." "Talk" reported city events that were usually overlooked by the newspapers. The first page of the column contained editorial "Notes and Comment." For these paragraphs, Andy made observations on daily events, trends, and social issues.

Ross demanded four things in his writers' work: accuracy, clarity, a casual approach, and an ability to poke fun at life in New York City. Andy's writing exhibited these requirements. He did not forget Professor Strunk's advice to omit needless words. He remembered Mr. Johns's statement: "Just say the words." Andy's paragraphs quickly earned a reputation for their lighthearted, perceptive style.

Since "Notes and Comment" were meant to be the opinion of the whole magazine, Andy wrote these paragraphs using the word *we* rather than *I*. His name did not appear as a byline to this column. Other articles he signed "E. B. White," "E. B. W.," or used a pseudonym. As Andy's responsibilities increased, he also wrote cartoon captions, light verse, drama reviews, and advertisements.

With Andy's well-written "Notes and Comment" at the front of each issue, *The New Yorker* flourished. Circulation increased, and more good writers joined the staff.

Andy was dependable in getting his work done, but he refused to settle in to steady hours. Once he even took a vacation to Maine without informing the office of his plans.

Even though Andy wrote for a very sophisticated magazine, he remained a quiet, modest individual. He avoided the parties attended by well-known writers, artists, and performers. One time, when he visited a friend's home and found a party in progress, he sneaked out a back door before anyone could notice him.

As a boy, Andy had worried about grown-up concerns, such as work and marriage. Now that he was an adult, he still worried about these things. Andy was especially reluctant to make commitments. In his work, he preferred to set his own schedule and wanted the freedom to come and go as he wished. In his dating relationships, he was even more wary of commitment.

Andy drew the cover illustration for the April 23, 1932, issue of The New Yorker.

For a while, Andy dated a woman he met in New York named Mary Osborn and, later, a secretary at *The New Yorker* named Rosanne Magdol. For Andy a date generally consisted of a long walk in the city. But marriage was never discussed. Andy was not ready to settle down.

About this time, Andy read Henry David Thoreau's book *Walden*. Thoreau wrote about his experiences while living alone at Walden Pond near Concord, Massachusetts. Andy shared Thoreau's preference for solitude and the peacefulness of nature. He carried the book with him and read it many times. Thoreau's words influenced Andy's thinking about life.

On May 1, 1929, Andy's first book was published. *The Lady Is Cold,* which contained 64 poems Andy had written, was well received.

Shortly after Andy began working for *The New Yorker,* he told a friend that Ross was looking for more editors. The friend told this to James Thurber, a writer who had sold several articles to *The New Yorker.* Andy barely knew Thurber, but set up an appointment for him to meet Ross.

Ross mistakenly believed that Andy and Thurber were close friends. Since Ross respected Andy's work, he readily hired Thurber as managing editor. Thurber and Andy shared a small office and soon did become good friends. The two men worked well together. Their contributions to *The New Yorker* were models of good writing.

Thurber liked to draw cartoons on yellow copy paper. He often sketched dogs, especially his pet Scottish terrier. Andy thought the drawings were good. But day after day, Thurber threw them away.

One day, Andy pulled a sketch out of the wastebasket, carefully traced over it with ink, and took it to the art editor. Ross and the art editors were not interested.

A self-portrait of
Thurber and dog.

One of James Thurber's many sketches: "A self-portrait of Thurber and dog"

Andy and Thurber collaborated on a book, *Is Sex Necessary?*, which made fun of the numerous texts written about sex by doctors and psychiatrists. Some of Thurber's drawings were used to illustrate the book.

Harold Ross discovered that readers liked Thurber's drawings in the book. He was embarrassed that he had not listened to Andy's advice. Soon, Thurber's drawings appeared in *The New Yorker*. The sketches proved to be very popular.

Katharine Angell

～☜☞ SIX ☜☞～

E. B. and Katharine

1929–1934

*T*he *New Yorker* owed much of its success to Katharine Angell's skills as an editor. In a gentle but persuasive manner she brought out the best in both new and experienced writers.

At home, though, Katharine's life was not so successful. Her marriage to attorney Ernest Angell was turbulent. Katharine worried about the effects of their arguments on their children, 12-year-old Nancy and 9-year-old Roger.

Meanwhile, through their work together at *The New Yorker*, Andy and Katharine became good friends. Andy sometimes wrote poems about Katharine.

In June 1928, when Katharine and her family were on vacation in France, Andy arranged to travel there too, in part, to see Katharine. Together they went canoeing on the Seine River.

After returning from France, Andy and Katharine decided it would be best if they did not socialize with each other. They would limit their discussions to work matters, they resolved. By winter Andy considered quitting his job at *The New Yorker* in order to separate himself from Katharine. But instead of quitting, he went to the Belgrade Lakes in Maine for a week. There he skated and tried to sort out his mixed-up feelings about love, work, and writing.

The Angells were striving to save their marriage, but their quarrels continued, and Katharine decided to separate from Ernest. Andy, along with James Thurber, helped Katharine move out. After several months, Katharine decided to get a divorce.

Since it was easier to get a divorce in Nevada than in New York, Katharine moved to Reno, Nevada. She stayed there for three months in order to comply with Nevada law. During that time, she and Andy wrote letters to each other.

While Katharine was in Nevada, Andy took a leave of absence from *The New Yorker* and retreated to Camp Otter in Ontario, where he had once worked as a camp counselor. He was delighted to see that the place had not changed much over the years. His friend Robert Hubbard now owned the camp. Andy envied Hubbard's involvement, and so the two men talked about becoming partners in the business.

While Andy was at Camp Otter, Katharine's divorce was finalized, and she returned to New York. Under a joint custody agreement, Nancy and Roger stayed with Ernest during the week and with Katharine on weekends and in the summer. To young Roger, it was a poor arrangement, as he wanted to be with his mother. Nancy, too, was upset, feeling rejected by her mother's actions.

Before Andy returned to New York, he and Hubbard reached an agreement, and Andy became part-owner of Camp Otter. Although his time at camp resulted in a business decision, Andy returned to Katharine and *The New Yorker* as unsettled as before.

Back at work together, Andy and Katharine's relationship became more serious. It wasn't long before they were discussing marriage. Andy hesitated, though. He wondered what people would think if he married a divorced woman who was seven years older than him and the mother of two children.

On November 13, 1929, Andy and Katharine were continuing their ongoing discussion about marriage. Katharine said something about her ivy plants.

"Oh, let the ivy rest!" Andy said. To his surprise, Katharine responded softly. Something in her manner made Andy realize that Katharine was "the girl for me."

Andy and Katharine decided to get married that very day. They applied for a marriage license at City Hall, looked at rings in a jewelry store, and ate lunch at a favorite restaurant. Then they drove 50 miles north to Bedford Village to get married. Katharine's dog, Daisy, went with them. The justice of the peace was unavailable, so Dr. A. R. Fulton performed the ceremony in the local Presbyterian church. Andy described his marriage as "the most beautiful decision of his life."

Andy and Katharine's marriage surprised many people, including Nancy and Roger. According to Nancy, the children didn't know about the wedding until their aunt read about it in the newspaper the next day. The mood in the Angell household was tense. Ernest had nothing good to say about Andy. The children quickly learned to avoid conflict by not mentioning Andy's name in their father's presence.

The children's first weekend with Andy and Katharine was difficult. Katharine needed to help her children adjust to her new marriage. The next summer, Katharine rented an apartment in Bedford Village, where she could devote more time to Nancy and Roger. Andy returned to Camp Otter for a few months. Although his hay fever still flared up in the summer, Andy kept busy helping parents and campers.

Nancy and Roger enjoyed the summer alone with their

mother. Gradually, the two children were coming to accept Andy. They were especially excited when they learned that Katharine and Andy were expecting a baby.

Andy was excited too. He sent Katharine a letter in which he pretended Daisy had written about the pregnancy: "White is beside himself and would have said more about it but is holding himself back, not wanting to appear ludicrous to a veteran mother." Sometimes Andy referred to the unborn child as "Serena," other times as "Little Joe."

Joel McCoun White was born on December 21, 1930. The delivery was difficult for Katharine and sickness forced her to spend the next six weeks in bed. During that time, Andy took care of Joel. Andy was apprehensive about his responsibilities as a father, yet filled with pride in his new son.

After a summer vacation at a rented cottage in Blue Hill, Maine, Katharine and Andy returned to *The New Yorker* in the fall of 1931 with renewed enthusiasm. Andy faithfully wrote the weekly "Notes and Comment" column. He contributed articles and "Talk of the Town" pieces, in addition to editing news-breaks and picture captions. A collection of the newsbreaks were published that year in the book *Ho Hum*.

Katharine became Ross's chief editorial adviser. She edited the works of many writers who later became famous, such as John Updike, Ogden Nash, Mary McCarthy, and John Cheever, not to mention E. B. White.

For the next two summers, Andy, Katharine, Nancy, Roger, and Joel returned to the rented cottage in Maine. These summers were relaxed and filled with family activities. Andy taught the children how to sail, in a light blue boat called *Faint Endeavor*. He also taught Nancy how to drive a car. The lessons went well, without a single argument. Andy spent a lot of time with Joel, a happy, active preschooler.

Katharine with her children, Joel, Nancy, and Roger, in Maine

One summer day in 1933, the Whites chartered a yacht and went out for a cruise. Toward evening, they anchored in a cove not far from Blue Hill. In the distance, beyond a stony pasture, Andy spied a barn. From the time he was a child with a stable in his backyard, Andy had been intrigued by barns.

The next day, Andy and Katharine drove through the North Brooklin area and located the barn. It was attached to an impressive two-story house and set on a 40-acre tract that extended to the cove. A "For Sale" sign stood in the yard. Using money they had saved over the years, the Whites bought the farm for 11,000 dollars.

Andy and Katharine kept their apartment in New York City

Katharine and Andy bought a farm with a house and attached barn—

and used the farm as a vacation home. The next summer, they returned to Maine to find flowers blooming and a garden full of strawberries, beans, and other vegetables that their care-taker had planted. But the farmwork was not left entirely to the hired help. Katharine loved to be in the garden, planting and weeding. After a while, she wrote articles about garden-ing for *The New Yorker.* Andy acquired five heifers and put the barn and pasture to use.

Throughout the early 1930s, *The New Yorker* was a literary and financial success, and the Whites prospered too. Even though the United States was suffering through the Great Depression, the magazine rarely mentioned it. Ross did not

shown here from the north in late summer—in Brooklin, Maine.

Minnie, the dachshund, and Andy at work in his New Yorker *office*

want *The New Yorker* to dwell on depressing or controversial subjects.

Ross's attempts to avoid controversy met with criticism. Ralph Ingersoll, editor of *Fortune* magazine, harshly accused Ross, Thurber, and Andy of failing to adequately confront problems of poverty and injustice that people faced as a result of the Depression. Ingersoll described Andy as "shy, frightened of life, often melancholy, always hypochondriac" and called his writing "gossamer."

It was no secret to Andy's family that he was a hypochondriac. It became difficult, both for doctors and relatives, to distinguish between Andy's real physical problems and his imagined ones. It was also true that Andy was shy and easily worried about things. From the time he was a young boy, fearful of being called upon in the school assembly, Andy avoided crowds and demanding social obligations. But his writing could hardly be considered light, airy, and insubstantial, as Ingersoll's attack had suggested.

The peace and self-confidence Andy had experienced during the early 1930s began to subside. Poor health plagued him. In addition to an upset stomach and the flu, he complained of physical ailments that the doctors could not diagnose.

Andy grew more depressed, feeling he had failed to produce a substantial written work. He took trips to South Carolina and Florida in an effort to get away from the distractions of home and work.

One evening Andy's face swelled. A doctor diagnosed the problem as a severe sunburn. Andy thought he might have a "tumor of the brain" or, at least, a spider bite.

The publication of his book *Every Day is Saturday* encouraged Andy. The book contained some of his "Notes and Comment" columns from 1928 to 1934. Words of praise appeared in the *Saturday Review of Literature,* the *New York Times,* the *New York American,* and even came from Andy's college professor, William Strunk.

The Astrid *in Tenant's Harbor, Maine*

ᏋᏃᎨᏗ SEVEN ᏋᏃᎨᏗ

Sorrow

1935–1937

In the spring of 1935, Andy purchased *Astrid,* a 30-foot cruising boat. With the help of two experienced yachtsmen, he sailed along the Maine coast to the farm at North Brooklin. That summer, he went deep-sea fishing and caught 300 pounds of cod and haddock.

Andy continued writing "Notes and Comment," anonymously, but he found the task difficult. "Even writing a letter seems an imposition," he told a friend. Andy's frustration grew when publishers rejected several of his poems, essays, and a proposed book about New York.

On August 13, 1935, Samuel White, Andy's 81-year-old father, died. Nancy and Roger had met Andy's parents during previous summers in Maine. Samuel had occasionally treated the children with gifts. When 15-year-old Roger learned of the death, he sent a sympathy card to Andy. Jessie White went to Washington, D.C., to stay with her daughter Clara.

A short time later, Andy and Katharine learned that Katharine was pregnant again. This time she was sick, and they feared a miscarriage. When their summer vacation ended, Katharine decided to stay in Maine for more rest. Andy felt compelled to return to New York to supervise the move from their small apartment in Greenwich Village to a house farther

BE MY VALENTINE!

Here in the house of Fred and Hattie,
Buttercups, Nicky, gup and platty,
Where Viking ships with crimson sails
Toss in the loud pre-breakfast gales,
And springtime's gentle hocus pocus
Thrives in a pot of purple crocus
That day of all is most divine
When I renew my VALENTINE!

A Valentine poem to Katharine from Andy

uptown. Andy and Katharine had picked out a spacious dwelling in the historic Turtle Bay Gardens, an attractive neighborhood of brownstone houses that shared a garden.

When Andy returned to New York, he left four-year-old Joel with Katharine. Nancy and Roger had already returned to their father in New York after spending the summer in Maine. Andy worried about Katharine and wrote to her often. He tried to cheer her with letters about their new house and details of packing He hired painters to brighten the rooms, bought new curtains, and bragged about the large bookshelves. Joel would have his own room. The house could also accommodate the White's live-in servants. Andy's only reservation about the move was that it might solidify their ties to the city.

The New Yorker was also in transition. Its offices on West 45th Street were too cramped. In the autumn of 1935, the magazine moved into several floors of a large red brick office building located only two blocks away. The building at 25 West 43rd Street was impressive, with marble wainscoting, hanging bronze lanterns, railed terraces, and many windows.

In September Katharine suffered a miscarriage. Andy was not with her at the time, and he grieved privately. He telephoned Nancy and Roger, who soberly received the news. In a letter to his brother, Andy said the event was "very disquieting and disturbing to both our spirits."

In the midst of these events, Andy also helped his mother close up her house in Mount Vernon. There were many details to work out, such as what to do with old pictures, sheet music, and Andy's piano.

Jessie White seemed to adjust well to the changes in her life, but her health was deteriorating. Andy noticed an "autumnal chill" in the bare house. Clara reminded Andy that their mother eagerly looked for mail each day.

Early in 1936, the *Saturday Review of Literature* offered Andy a job as an editor. Andy had high regard for the magazine and was looking for a change in his life. But he laughed at the idea of being an editor.

"I can't edit the side of a barn," he replied to Christopher Morley, the *Review*'s contributing editor. Andy feared he would totally ruin the magazine. He described himself as a "literary defective" with "whimsical" health.

On May 1, 1936, Andy learned that his mother had inoperable cancer. The doctor predicted that she would live only a few more months. The news came as a terrible shock to Andy and his brothers and sisters.

Andy hurried to Washington, D.C., to be with his mother. By the time he arrived, Jessie was critically ill. The next day, she seemed to revive, but her recovery was brief. Jessie White died that evening, only two weeks after the cancer had been diagnosed.

After his mother's funeral, Andy walked through the cemetery where both his mother and father were buried. Andy could hardly believe that in just one year both of his parents had died. Andy found comfort at the Belgrade Lakes in Maine. He watched fish swim in the pond and listened to the birds call. This was the one place where things had not changed.

Andy was unhappy. He was angry at Ross, who had printed an outdated and inappropriate "Notes and Comment" column while the Whites were on vacation the prior summer. Even so, his essays were very popular. A favorite was his tribute to the Model T Ford in "Farewell, My Lovely!"

Andy was also sensitive to the continued attacks of Ralph Ingersoll. In 1937 President Franklin D. Roosevelt proposed "packing" the Supreme Court by increasing the number of justices. Roosevelt wanted to appoint justices who agreed with him in order to save his New Deal programs from being declared unconstitutional. Andy wrote a strong editorial criticizing the president. Ingersoll complained that Andy's attitude was complacent. Andy wearied from the debate.

His biggest complaint, though, was that he still had to anonymously write "Notes and Comment" with the editorial "we," rather than in a more personal tone. But the column was considered one of *The New Yorker*'s strengths, and Ross was unwilling to change its format.

By the end of May 1937, Andy was ready to quit. He didn't know how to explain his feelings to Katharine. Whenever he mentioned his plans, she seemed to bristle with anger. But in spite of Katharine's apparent displeasure, Andy decided to take a year's leave of absence. He told Katharine about it in a letter. He called it "My Year."

"I am not satisfied with the use I am making of my talents," Andy wrote to Katharine. He had several writing projects in mind, but he did not disclose his ideas, even to Katharine. "My plan is to have none," he continued. He asked for the liberty to come and go, free of family routines. Andy admitted that his year off was selfish. "But that's the way the art goes," he wrote.

Katharine accepted Andy's decision, but it troubled her. He had been absent before—when she was pregnant with Joel, on his trips to Maine and Florida, even during a painful miscarriage. But this time was different. Andy seemed to be floundering.

Andy in his office at The New Yorker

&ce✿ EIGHT ✿ce

A Change of Pace

1937–1942

Andy's leave of absence began with a 12-day cruise off the coast of Maine. Then Katharine and Joel joined him at the farm for the summer. Katharine continued her editing, while Andy puttered around the farm.

After Katharine and Joel returned to New York, Andy set a schedule to write every day between nine and one o'clock. But instead of writing, he went fishing, cleaned out the garden, and tinkered with farm tools. By the end of October, all he had written was a very personal poem, which he immediately filed away in a drawer.

That winter, Andy returned to New York. His reunion with Katharine did not go well. By Christmas they were both sick and argumentative. Andy once again retreated to Maine, this time taking seven-year-old Joel with him for a week-long vacation.

At first Andy was too preoccupied with a sore throat to attend much to Joel. Joel didn't seem to mind. He quickly made friends with the neighbor boys and took off skiing. But as Andy began to feel better, he and Joel started to enjoy the outdoors together. They skated on the frog pond and held a private picnic in the back seat of a friend's Dodge touring car. Even though it was cold, the two had fun.

During this week in Maine, Andy gave serious thought to his life. Katharine was right, he realized. "A single person can act aimlessly," he wrote to her, "but where lives mingle and merge there has to be a scheme in advance."

Katharine and Andy relax with Minnie in Maine.

Andy proposed that they all move to Maine for the whole year. Although she liked going to Maine in the summer, Katharine was content with her life in New York. She enjoyed her work as an associate editor and earned a good salary. Her writers and coworkers urged her not to leave.

By this time, Nancy had graduated from Bryn Mawr and was in graduate school studying biology. Roger was at Harvard, majoring in English. Like Andy, Roger was a writer. Andy encouraged Roger's writing and even helped get one of Roger's poems published. Katharine did not worry about the effect of their move on Nancy and Roger. But she was reluctant to transfer seven-year-old Joel from his private school in the city to a two-room country school.

Most of all, though, Katharine loved Andy. She wanted to be with him. So she decided to move to Maine with him. *The New Yorker* agreed to mail articles to the farm, where Katharine could continue editing on a part-time basis.

When the news spread that Andy was leaving *The New Yorker,* other publications offered him work. *Harper's Magazine* proposed a monthly column called "One Man's Meat," which Andy could write while living in Maine. Andy agreed to write the 2,500-word column for $300 each month. The essays would carry his byline and be written in the first person.

Ross tried to get Andy to return to *The New Yorker.* Andy finally agreed to edit newsbreaks and to submit articles from Maine.

The Whites officially moved to the farm in the summer of 1938. Despite the inconveniences typical of country life— frozen water pipes in the winter, sick animals, and the nine miles into town—Andy loved the farm. The Whites remodeled the farmhouse, providing Andy and Katharine with separate studies. Books lined the walls and a large wood-burning stove dominated the kitchen. The shed connecting the house and barn was filled with chopped wood.

Andy took special pleasure in the barn—his own barn—which he filled with chickens, cows, sheep, geese, and even a few pigs. He bought 84 day-old chicks to raise. Since he was not an experienced farmer, he thought that many of the chicks would die before maturity. To his surprise, only three chicks died.

When the chicks began producing, Andy was overwhelmed. At the rate of 20 eggs a day, the Whites could not consume all the produce. Embarrassed, Andy asked the local grocer to market the extra eggs.

Rural life offered the Whites less privacy than city living.

Andy tends sheep on his farm.

Katharine and Andy feed their sheep.

In New York City, neighbors barely knew each other. But in the country and the nearby communities of North Brooklin and Blue Hills, life was different. Neighbors greeted each other in passing, often pausing to engage in small talk. Farmers kept track of vehicles on the country roads and could report who was or wasn't home. Andy felt his life was under greater scrutiny.

Andy included anecdotes about the farm in his monthly columns for *Harper's*. He reported ownership of 15 sheep, 148 layer hens, 3 geese, 6 roosters, a dog, a cat, a pig, "and a captive mouse." The Whites kept a large garden of "apples, pumpkins, squash, potatoes, and cow beets." They canned and preserved most of the produce. Andy's fishing excursions yielded haddock for chowder and mackerel for canning.

The countryside stirred with deer, foxes, ducks, and other wildlife. Local farmers asked Andy to join them when they went hunting, but he excused himself, claiming poor eyesight.

Joel readily adjusted to the country school. On nice days, he walked the two and a half miles to class, his blue lunch pail in hand.

In addition to writing "One Man's Meat" and occasional pieces for *The New Yorker*, Andy worked on several other projects. One was his story about Stuart, the mouselike boy. Ever since his dream many years earlier, Andy had been writing new adventures. When Joel or his cousins had asked for a story, Andy opened a desk drawer and pulled out an episode about Stuart.

In the mid 1930s, Andy had begun to compile the stories into a children's book. At first he had called his character Stuart Ades, but then he changed the name to Stuart Little.

Andy had made several attempts to write the story's beginning. He wrote and rewrote the paragraphs in longhand on yellow copy paper, crossing out words and continually making changes. Then he typed it up and set it aside.

Andy returned to the story of Stuart Little in 1938. At that time, Katharine was reviewing children's books for *The New Yorker*, and review copies littered the farmhouse. Out of curiosity, Andy read a few of the books. He was impressed with the broad range of subjects covered in children's literature, but he was put off when a writer was condescending to readers. Andy thought "that it must be a lot of fun to write for children—reasonably easy work, perhaps even important work."

Andy wrote an essay for *Harper's* expressing his views on children's books. Anne Carroll Moore, the highly respected children's librarian at the New York Public Library, read the column and urged Andy to write a children's book. Andy decided to try out *Stuart Little* and sent the incomplete manuscript to several publishers.

Eugene Saxton, Andy's editor at the publishing house of Harper and Brothers, expressed interest in *Stuart Little* and asked Andy to finish the story. Andy replied that he would try to complete the book for a fall 1939 release, but he couldn't promise to have it done. "Everything depends on whether the finished product turns out pleasing to mine eye. I would rather wait a year than publish a bad children's book, as I have too much respect for children."

Andy was busy producing other books, and *Stuart Little* was again set aside. *The Fox of Peapack*, a collection of Andy's poems, appeared in October 1938, followed five months later by a collection of satirical essays in the volume *Quo Vadimus? Or the Case for the Bicycle*. In addition to writing and farming, Andy took his family on frequent trips to New York City and even a journey to Florida in hopes of relieving Joel's asthma.

Meanwhile, trouble stirred in Europe. Adolf Hitler, the German dictator, threatened to overthrow the governments of weaker nations. In March 1938, German soldiers invaded Austria, and by March 1939, all of Czechoslovakia was occupied by Germany. Britain and France were poised to fight back. The United States anxiously watched, debating whether to get involved.

Andy's usually lighthearted essays took a sobering turn. The fragile nature of world peace troubled him. Even when he was on the barn roof fastening shingles, he thought of war.

Germany invaded Poland on September 1, 1939. On September 3, 1939, England declared war on Germany. Although the Whites did not regularly attend church, that day they sought its comfort. In the evening, they listened to the king of England's speech on the radio.

Andy was far away from the war in Europe, but he felt its tension. Coast Guardsmen walked along the beach. Patrol planes buzzed overhead. At night the Whites turned out their lights and drew their window shades for local blackouts, precautions against air raids. Supplies that were needed for the war effort, such as tires and scrap metal, were rationed.

President Franklin Roosevelt warned Americans to be prepared for involvement in the war. He spoke of the "four freedoms"—freedom of speech and freedom of religion, freedom from fear and freedom from want.

In 1940 Eugene Saxton asked Andy to write a book for Harper and Brothers about American heritage and democracy. The book was never completed, but Andy's efforts resulted in the important essay "Freedom."

A few months later, Anne Morrow Lindbergh, wife of the famed aviator Charles Lindbergh, published a book protesting the United States' involvement in the war. Andy responded with a stinging essay criticizing Lindbergh's book.

Ironically, in the midst of these troubling years, Andy and Katharine compiled an anthology of humor. *A Subtreasury of American Humor,* released in 1941, contained fables, tales, parodies, and other humorous pieces. Readers appreciated the Whites' choice of humor. The book sold 15,000 copies in just one month.

In the summer of 1941, Andy took 10-year-old Joel to the Belgrade Lakes. It was a special time for father and son. Together they explored the streams and fished. Andy watched with pride as Joel mastered the outboard motor on their boat. In his monthly *Harper's* column, Andy shared the emotion of seeing Joel experience the things that were still vivid memories from his own boyhood. "Once More to the Lake" became one of Andy's most popular essays. This essay and others from

Roger and Joel on the North Brooklin beach in 1940

the *Harper's* column were collected in the book *One Man's Meat*. The book was temporarily banned by the army and navy, however, because of the political statements Andy made in some of the essays.

On December 7, 1941, Japan bombed Pearl Harbor, Hawaii. The United States could no longer be neutral. The next day, the United States declared war on Japan.

As a young man during World War I, Andy had struggled to find a way to effectively serve his country. Now he felt the same frustration.

In his essays and editorials, Andy shared his convictions about freedom. He believed that sometimes it was necessary to risk life for a government that protected individual freedoms. He contrasted the plight of those people being denied basic freedoms with his own life, so full of liberties.

Garth Williams drew Stuart Little, who was just about the size of a mouse, looked like a mouse, and acted like a mouse.

ᥡ NINE ᥡ

Stuart and Margalo
1943–1946

By 1943 five years had passed since the Whites' move to Maine. In addition to livestock and garden vegetables, Andy had produced several books and over 50 essays for his column called "One Man's Meat." Publishers vied for his attention. Ross kept asking Andy to return to New York. *Stuart Little* was under consideration for publication by Harper and Brothers.

The family was growing up too. Joel was almost a teenager, ready to enroll in Exeter, a boarding school in New Hampshire. Nancy had married in 1941; Roger in 1942. Both couples were busy with their jobs and establishing homes.

It might have been a happy time for Andy, but the war continued to weigh heavily on his mind. In 1942 he had offered to help create a pamphlet commissioned by President Roosevelt on the four freedoms. For Andy, this was a tangible way to serve his country.

Andy believed that international peace could be attained through a world government. Hesitantly at first, then more boldly and frequently, he expressed this thought in his essays and articles. He wrote *The Wild Flag,* developing the idea of a world government.

Sensing Andy's desire to write more about the war, Ross again urged Andy to return to *The New Yorker.* Magazine sales lagged. Ross knew that readers liked Andy's writing and that circulation might rally if he contributed on a more regular basis. Ross offered Andy more money if he would return to New York.

Katharine was ready to return to the city, but Andy was not. He wasn't convinced that *The New Yorker*'s "Notes and Comment" column was the proper forum for expressing views on world government. He hesitated to present his personal views as the opinion of the editorial staff. Furthermore, *The*

Andy and Katharine review a writing project together.

New Yorker was a humor magazine and tended to avoid controversy. Andy feared that the magazine might be embarrassed by his idealistic notion of a world government. Finally, Andy was not ready to give up the farm, his regular dips in Allen Cove, or the animals in the barn. But Ross eventually prevailed. Andy wrote his last column for *Harper's* in March 1943.

The decision to return to New York further taxed Andy's fragile emotional state. In his letters, he frequently complained about his health. He appeared to be lacking direction or purpose in his work. A doctor was treating him with strychnine, apparently for depression.

Katharine was recovering from surgery and was, herself, feeling poorly. Andy's depression worsened, and he suffered a nervous breakdown. Writing was difficult. Andy complained about his head. He listened to old records on the phonograph to calm his nerves.

His depression continued, off and on, into the winter months. He underwent neurological tests to diagnose his condition. One doctor determined that Andy had an excess of red blood cells caused by hyperventilating.

The Whites did not sell their farm, but in November of 1944, they moved into an apartment in Greenwich Village, close to the place where Andy had lived in the 1920s. Andy's good memories of the neighborhood cheered him. He suddenly felt healthy and inspired again.

For the next eight weeks, Andy worked on the *Stuart Little* manuscript. He often wrote in the morning, seated near a window on the top floor of the apartment.

Since Eugene Saxton had died, Andy was working with Ursula Nordstrom, another editor at Harper and Brothers. Nordstrom was apprehensive about Andy's book. Just because a person could write well for adults did not mean that he could write a good children's story. But after Nordstrom read *Stuart Little,* she knew she didn't need to worry.

Stuart Little is the story of a boy who looks like a mouse and grows only a little taller than two inches. Stuart recovers his mother's diamond ring from the bathtub drain, finds lost Ping-Pong balls, and crawls into the piano to unstick piano keys for his brother.

Stuart experiences a variety of troubles and adventures, including an exciting boat race. Margalo, a pretty bird, comes to the Littles' house. She and Stuart become good friends.

When two cats plot to capture Margalo, a pigeon warns Margalo with an anonymous note. Fearing for her life, Margalo leaves without a word to anyone. It is spring, so she heads north.

Stuart is sad. He searches for Margalo, who once rescued him from a garbage scow in the ocean. He leaves home, using a miniature car given to him by a dentist. As the story ends,

Margalo carries Stuart high above the East River, saving him from being dumped from a garbage scow into the ocean.

Stuart is heading north, which he expects he'll be doing for the rest of his life. "But the sky was bright, and he somehow felt he was headed in the right direction."

Anne Carroll Moore, the librarian who had encouraged Andy to write a children's book, read a review copy of *Stuart Little*. She didn't like the book and wrote a 14-page letter advising Andy to withdraw the story. Other people expressed reservations about *Stuart Little*, too. Some said the ending was too inconclusive. But Andy did not back down. He believed that children could easily accept the shift from reality to make-believe.

Some readers wondered if Stuart ever returns home or finds Margalo. Andy replied, "Stuart's journey symbolizes the continuing journey that everybody takes—in search of what is perfect and unattainable." But on another occasion, Andy said that he was sick at the time he penned the last chapters of the book and was "under the impression that I had only a short time to live, and so I may have brought the story to a more abrupt close than I would have under different circumstances."

Stuart Little was published in 1945 by Harper and Brothers. Garth Williams illustrated the text with almost 90 sketches. Despite Moore's pessimism, the book was a best-seller. The first printing of 50,000 copies sold so well that Harper issued a second printing only two weeks later. The book sold 100,000 copies by December 1946.

With the publication of *Stuart Little,* Andy's life at age 46 took a new turn. He was not only an essayist and humorist, but he was also a children's author. As Stuart might have noted, Andy "was headed in the right direction."

Andy, at home in his barn, holds two young lambs.

TEN

Politics and Controversy
1947–1951

Early in 1947, Andy wrote to his brother, "I'm glad to report that even now, at this late day, a blank sheet of paper holds the greatest excitement there is for me—more promising than a silver cloud, prettier than a little red wagon."

Andy wrote insightful, often humorous, accounts of daily events. After a visit to the Bronx Zoo, he wrote a beautiful essay about the birth of twin fawns. Another time he wrote about the death of a pig on the farm. While spending a week at the Algonquin Hotel, he penned "Here Is New York," an essay later published as a small book.

Sometimes writing about daily events made those events less enjoyable for Andy. Instead of being able to relax and enjoy a view or an experience, he was mentally taking notes on it for a future article.

Andy lapsed into another period of depression, and a psychiatrist advised him to write less. This helped for a while, but Andy felt compelled to write.

Andy told his brother that he even considered writing a

biography about Katharine. Andy clearly admired his wife's quiet achievements as an editor at *The New Yorker*. She was an exceptional woman with keen editing skills, Andy knew. She had guided many beginning writers on to publication and fame. But Katharine had rarely received recognition for her work. Andy didn't think this was fair.

Following World War II, the United Nations formed and built its offices near the Whites' Turtle Bay apartment. Andy wondered whether this organization would fulfill his hopes for a world government. Occasionally he observed a United Nations meeting and reported on it in *The New Yorker*.

Suspicion also followed the war. The House Un-American Activities Committee sought to expose suspected Communists. Ten Hollywood screenwriters refused to tell the committee whether they were members of the Communist Party, so their producers fired them. The *New York Herald Tribune* supported the firing.

Andy called the committee's questioning "loyalty testing and thought control." While he did not support Communism, he thought it unfair to fire people for their beliefs. In a letter to the *Herald Tribune*, Andy called himself "a member of a party of one."

Even in a serious letter such as this, Andy used humor. He wrote, "I can only assume that your editorial writer, in a hurry to get home for Thanksgiving, tripped over the First Amendment and thought it was the office cat."

The *Tribune* editors said Andy was dangerous. Supreme Court Justice Felix Frankfurter praised Andy for his remarks. The Whites' mailbox overflowed with Communist literature.

Andy's reputation as a writer spread. Three universities— Dartmouth, Yale, and the University of Maine—awarded him honorary degrees. Andy dreaded the public appearances.

On June 22, 1948, Yale University awarded honorary degrees to these people. E. B. White stands in the center of the back row. The future president Eisenhower stands in the front row, second from the left.

At Dartmouth, he became nervous and sick the night before the graduation. The next day, he suffered through awkward conversations, posing for photographs, and waiting in line. When his name was called, Andy walked to the platform. A school official slipped a long white hood over his head. Andy forgot to secure the hood to a button on his gown. As he sat down, the hood caught on the man sitting next to him.

Embarrassed, Andy felt certain that all the students witnessed his mishap.

In 1949 Andy once again resigned from writing "Notes and Comment" for *The New Yorker,* although he continued contributing articles. In his essays, he complained about the shape of taxicabs, worried about the atomic bomb, and wrangled over noise levels.

Holiday magazine asked Andy to take a trip across the United States and write an account about his journey. Andy started on the trip, but soon became discouraged by all the fast-paced traffic. He returned home after just a few weeks. The assignment was later given to John Steinbeck, who wrote about his trip in *Travels with Charley.*

At Thanksgiving the Whites were delighted to have their children and grandchildren home. Joel had followed in the steps of his father and uncles, attending Cornell. After two years, he transferred to M.I.T. to pursue a degree in naval architecture. Nancy and her husband came with their three children; Roger and his wife had a daughter. Andy was an attentive grandfather, listening carefully to the children and treating each one as an important individual. The family had a fun time together. They ate fish, wore silly hats, and played games.

On December 6, 1951, Harold Ross died during surgery for lung cancer. Although he had been sick for several years, the news stunned *The New Yorker* staff. Andy wrote a tribute to Ross for *The New Yorker.* He now recalled how Ross had ended his conversations with the words "All right. God bless you." In his tribute, Andy wrote, "with much love in our heart, we say, for everybody, 'All right, Ross. God bless you!'"

William Shawn, an editor at the magazine, took over Ross's duties. Andy and Katharine liked Shawn and his easygoing manner.

Andy plays baseball with his granddaughter, Martha White, above, *and writes in his study in Maine,* left.

Charlotte calls a meeting of the animals in the barn cellar to come up with a new slogan for her web.

❧❦ ELEVEN ❦❧

Charlotte and Wilbur

1952–1955

In the fall of 1949, Andy had told an editor at Harper and Brothers, "My next book is in sight. I look at it every day. I keep it in a carton, as you would a kitten."

About a year and a half later, Andy informed Ursula Nordstrom that he had completed the children's book, but had "put it away for a while to ripen." The book was *Charlotte's Web,* a story about a pig, a spider, and a farm.

It was natural for Andy to write about barn animals. As a child, the stable had been one of his favorite places. As an adult, his own barn housed an assortment of geese, pigs, chickens, cows, and sheep.

One aspect of raising livestock troubled Andy, however. Every year he raised a pig, faithfully feeding and caring for it, only to butcher it when it was fully grown. Andy was uncomfortable with this process. He felt that he had not been reliable to the pig.

This discomfort led Andy to create Wilbur, the pig in *Charlotte's Web.* Somehow, Wilbur would be spared from the butcher's knife.

One day at the farm, Andy found a spider in the outhouse. Using a lamp with a long extension cord, he watched the spider build webs and lay a big egg sac. This gave Andy an idea for saving Wilbur.

When it was time for the Whites to return to New York, Andy removed both the egg sac and the spider from the outhouse, carefully placing them in a candy box for the move to the city.

The spider soon died. But when the eggs hatched, little spiders migrated all over the room.

Andy spent a year researching spiders. He wrote out a list of questions. "How many eggs?" "When will they hatch?"

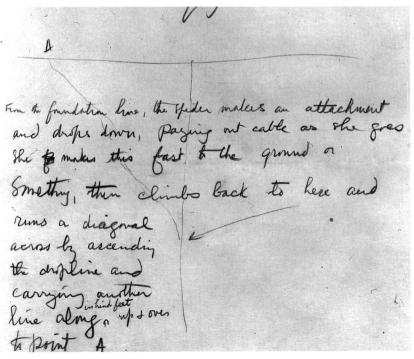

As he researched spiders for Charlotte's Web, Andy made notes about how a spider spins a web.

Andy made a sketch of the barnyard to help him as he wrote Charlotte's Web.

"When will the female die after egg laying?" He consulted science books and experts to learn the answers.

He also drew sketches of Zuckerman's barn and of the spider he named Charlotte. He listed words that Charlotte might spin in her web, and made another list of spider parts. He learned about sedentary spiders and wandering spiders, dry web thread and sticky thread. "Charlotte is near-sighted," he wrote in one of his notes.

On January 19, 1951, Andy finished the first draft of his story. The manuscript contained 17 chapters, beginning with a narrative about Wilbur in Zuckerman's barn. But, as Andy

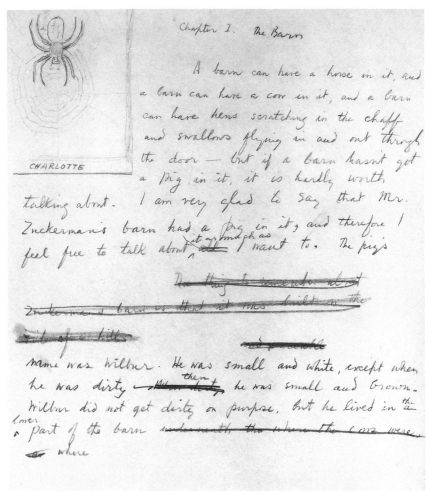

In one of the first versions of Charlotte's Web, *Andy begins the story by describing the barn.*

told Ursula Nordstrom, he didn't feel comfortable with it yet. He rewrote the beginning of the story several times. He couldn't decide whether to begin with a description of Wilbur or with Mr. Arable pulling on his boots and going out to the barn.

Andy let the manuscript rest for a while. When he returned to it, he shifted the focus of the beginning to Fern Arable. Through her eyes, the reader would be led into the barn. This required five new chapters and more editing.

① *table for breakfast.*

"Where's Papa going with that ax?" said Fern to
her mother ~~as they sat down to breakfast.~~ They were ~~in setting~~ *setting the* in
~~the kitchen having breakfast.~~

"Out to the hoghouse," replied Mrs. Arable. "Some
pigs were born last night."

"I don't see why he needs an ax," continued Fern,
who was only eight. ~~years old.~~

"Well," said her mother, ~~there were eleven~~ *the pig* ~~pigs were born, and~~ one of ~~them~~ is a runt ~~just~~ *It's very small, and* ~~a little bit of a~~ *doesn't amount to much.* ~~thing.~~ Your father will have to do away with it. It's no good."

"Do away with it?" shrieked Fern, "You mean kill
it? Just because it's smaller than the others?"

Mrs. Arable ~~helped herself to~~ put her spoon down
on her plate. "Don't yell, Fern!" she said. "Your father is
~~doing what is~~ right. The pig would probably die anyway." ~~damn~~

Fern slid out of her chair, and ran outdoors ~~toward~~
~~making no noise at all.~~ *The grass was wet and the earth smelled* ~~just before she reached.~~ ~~The grass was cool and damp~~ *of springtime.*
~~and her father. The grass was wet with dew and her~~
by the time
sneakers were ~~soaking wet before~~ she caught up with ~~him.~~ *her father.*

"Please don't kill it!" she sobbed. "It's unfair.'"

Mr. Arable stopped walking.

"Fern," said ~~her father,~~ *he* gently, "you will have to
learn to control yourself."

In the final version of Charlotte's Web, *Andy begins the book with Fern saving a newborn pig.*

One day Andy walked into the office of Harper and Brothers. "I've brought you a new manuscript," he announced, handing Ursula Nordstrom the finished book.

Charlotte's Web begins with Fern Arable pleading with her father to save a weak newborn pig. Mr. Arable spares the pig and gives it to Fern. She promptly names it Wilbur.

Garth Williams drew the illustrations for Charlotte's Web. *Here Fern feeds Wilbur his first breakfast.*

By the time Wilbur is five weeks old, he is too big to stay with the Arables. Reluctantly, Fern sells Wilbur to her uncle, Homer Zuckerman, who has a farm nearby.

The barn is a wonderful place, smelling of hay, manure, grain, and axle grease. Children swing from the long rope in the hayloft. But Wilbur is not happy there.

A fast-talking goose persuades Wilbur to escape from the barnyard, and an exciting chase ensues. Mr. Zuckerman finally entices Wilbur back into the barn with a pail of slops. The goose warns Wilbur that he will lose his freedom. But Wilbur prefers the security of the barn.

Wilbur is lonely. One night he hears an unfamiliar voice. "Do you want a friend, Wilbur?" the voice asks.

The next day, Wilbur finds Charlotte, a spider, high in the corner of a doorway. She explains to Wilbur how she traps flies in her web for food. Wilbur wonders if he will like her.

Wilbur finds out that he is being fattened for butchering. "I don't want to die!" he cries. "Save me, somebody! Save me!" Charlotte promises to save Wilbur.

One night, while the animals are asleep, Charlotte spins the words SOME PIG in her web. The next morning, the hired man sees the words in the dew-covered web. Soon, people are streaming into the barn to see Wilbur and the words in the web.

Charlotte spins more words in her web: TERRIFIC and RADIANT. Even though she is beginning to tire, she is determined to save Wilbur. In the fall, Mr. Zuckerman enters Wilbur in the county fair, and Charlotte goes along too.

Templeton, a rat, finds a word on a discarded newspaper and brings it to Charlotte. The word is HUMBLE.

"That's Wilbur all over," Charlotte declares, and she spins her last word in the web. During the night, she climbs to a high corner in the fair barn to work on her "magnum opus." In the morning, Wilbur sees Charlotte's egg sac hanging in the barn. The sac contains 514 eggs that will hatch in the spring. Charlotte is very tired.

When the Zuckermans and Arables arrive, they are delighted to see Charlotte's new word. But their joy turns to disappointment when they see a blue ribbon hanging on the pen of another pig.

Then, to everyone's surprise, the judges call the Zuckermans and Wilbur to the grandstand for a special award. The announcer says many nice things about Wilbur. Wilbur is nervous and faints. Templeton bites Wilbur's tail, instantly reviving the pig. A judge puts a medal around Wilbur's neck and awards Mr. Zuckerman 25 dollars.

Charlotte is satisfied. Her friend has been saved from the butcher's knife. But her own life is almost over. Wilbur is grateful to Charlotte for what she has done. He is sad that she is too weak to return to Zuckerman's barn. Wilbur takes Charlotte's egg sac back to Zuckerman's barn. The next day, Charlotte dies alone in the fair barn.

In the spring, baby spiders hatch from the egg sac. One by one they leave the barn, carried by balloons of spider silk. Three of Charlotte's daughters stay in the barn. Wilbur has new friends.

The story concludes: "It is not often that someone comes along who is a true friend and a good writer. Charlotte was both."

Garth Williams, who had illustrated *Stuart Little,* also drew the sketches for *Charlotte's Web.* Williams had difficulty drawing a spider that Andy liked. Andy sent Williams the book *American Spiders* by Willis J. Gertsch and suggested that the illustrator not worry about showing Charlotte's facial expressions. In the end, Andy was very pleased with the illustrations.

When *Charlotte's Web* appeared in bookstores in October of 1952, it was an immediate success. Sales were even better than Andy had anticipated. Fan letters, reviews, and awards poured in.

Charlotte's web hangs over one terrific pig.

Andy receives the Presidential Medal of Freedom.

❧ TWELVE ❧

Fame

1956–1967

The overwhelming popularity of *Charlotte's Web* surprised even its author. Children and adults flooded Andy with fan mail requesting pictures, autographs, and answers to questions. He graciously replied to the letters, even though it took much of his time. He liked to tell young readers about his farm and animals.

Sometimes readers tried to find hidden meanings in *Charlotte's Web*. To this Andy replied, "Just relax. Any attempt to find allegorical meanings is bound to end disastrously, for no meanings are in there. I ought to know."

Andy was not comfortable with fame. He was amazed at the boldness of curious fans who would arrive uninvited at his farmyard in Maine. He was asked to join literary organizations, participate in research projects, and speak at public events. He turned down these requests. "I am incapable of making a speech."

Andy received more honorary degrees, this time from Harvard University and Colby College in Maine. He turned down several other degrees due to scheduling conflicts.

Throughout his career, Andy was awarded numerous medals and certificates. For *Charlotte's Web,* Andy earned the Newbery Honor in 1953, a runner-up for "the most distinguished contribution" to American children's literature in the previous year. But Andy said that awards were "not very much fun or satisfaction and I would rather have a nice drink of ginger ale, usually."

Poor health contributed to the let-down feeling he experienced after *Charlotte's Web* was published. He suffered from shingles. Katharine had the mumps; they both had the flu. Andy seemed to complain of having almost any illness he heard about. Katharine sympathized with Andy's distresses and, likewise, claimed undiagnosed problems of her own. In addition to their ailments, they mourned the deaths of Katharine's sister and aunt.

In the spring of 1955, the Whites traveled to England. But instead of enjoying the vacation, they worried about the British railway strike, complained about the way people talked, and generally had a miserable time.

As Katharine's health worsened, it became more difficult for her to work. Ever since their return to *The New Yorker* in 1943, the Whites had continued to take vacations several times a year, usually to Maine. In 1957 Andy and Katharine decided to move back to Maine year-round. Slowly the Whites cut back on their work at *The New Yorker,* a semi-retirement.

Being back at the farm brightened Andy's spirits. Joel and his family lived nearby, and the grandchildren often came to visit. When he wanted to write, Andy retreated to the boathouse, which offered a peaceful view of the cove.

One day a friend at Cornell sent Andy a copy of William Strunk's book, *The Elements of Style.* Strunk had died, but his book remained an important guide to students of English.

Andy wrote an essay about Strunk and his book. Macmillan publishers noticed the essay and asked Andy to write a new introduction for the book. Before their negotiations were over, Andy had agreed to revise *The Elements of Style*. Andy spent a year working on the book. He added a chapter on style, deleted Strunk's chapter on misspelled words, and added new examples of the grammar rules.

Andy's own essays were examples of good writing. He often wrote about nature and acknowledged Thoreau's influence in a tribute written on the 100th anniversary of the publication of *Walden* in 1954. Rachel Carson, a writer and marine biologist, admired Andy's writing style and ideas. In 1957 a trial was held in New York regarding the spraying of DDT. Carson suggested that Andy report on the trial in *The New Yorker.* She believed that more people would pay attention to the contamination problem if a well-known writer like E. B. White wrote about it.

Andy was in Maine at the time of the trial. So he wrote back to Carson, urging her to write the article about DDT. In the end, Carson wrote a series of articles about contamination, which were published in *The New Yorker.* These articles were again published in 1962 as part of Carson's important book, *Silent Spring.* A stern quote by Andy appears in the beginning of the book.

Andy's own writings also warned about the dangers of society's careless treatment of the earth. In 1959 and 1960, he edited a series of articles on environmental pollution. He also questioned the wisdom of weapons testing, although he did not favor disarmament.

In 1960 the National Institute of Arts and Letters awarded Andy a gold medal for Essay and Criticism. Andy did not attend the ceremony to receive the gold medal.

In a letter to a friend, Andy asked, "Incidentally, where

does a man keep a gold medal? This one just makes me uneasy. I tried it in a bottom drawer and it seemed needlessly obscure. I tried it on the table in the hall and it seemed ostentatious....I see no solution to medals and don't really enjoy them."

What Andy desired, more than medals, was for Katharine to be in good health. She was in and out of doctor's offices and hospitals, undergoing surgery for a blocked artery, an appendectomy, and treatment for a rare skin disease. Cortisone

James Thurber and Andy White in the 1950s

Katharine White in the 1950s

medication weakened her bones, and it pained Andy to see Katharine's stooped figure leaning on a walker for support. Nursing attendants came to the farm. Andy declined invitations to special events on account of his wife's health.

In his sixties, Andy became more depressed. The death of his sister Marion made him more conscious of his own mortality. The deaths of other relatives and friends added to his gloom. He felt old and figured he did not have much time left. He began donating manuscripts and other memorabilia from his life to a special collection at Cornell University.

In 1961 a young fan asked Andy why he hadn't produced another children's book. In frustration Andy suggested that children should quit writing to him so that he would have more time to write a book. He complained that four years earlier he had begun researching a book, but he never had sufficient time to finish it.

Andy did produce a book in 1962 called *The Points of My Compass,* a collection of essays that had previously appeared in *The New Yorker.* But this book did little to encourage him.

By 1963 Andy's health was worse, and he was writing less. He worried about Katharine, their medical bills, and whether he was capable of sailing a boat anymore. The result was a nervous breakdown.

One day in July 1963, a Western Union operator called with a telegram for Andy. Katharine took the message because Andy was bathing. The telegram announced that President Kennedy had selected Andy to receive the Presidential Medal of Freedom. Katharine was so surprised that she asked the operator if the call was a practical joke. The operator sternly assured her that it was not.

Before the award ceremony occurred, President Kennedy was assassinated. Andy wrote Kennedy's obituary for *The New Yorker.* President Lyndon Johnson presented the medals in December, but Andy did not attend, claiming that Katharine was too sick to leave. Later, Senator Edmund Muskie of Maine awarded the medal to Andy at a special ceremony. The president's citation described Andy: "An essayist whose concise comment on men and places has revealed to yet another age the vigor of the English sentence."

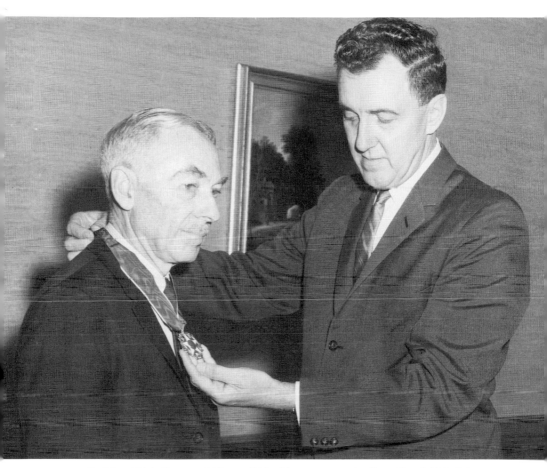

In May 1964, Senator Edmund Muskie presents the Presidential Medal of Freedom to E. B. White.

Although Andy generally disdained medals, this one was special to him. He felt honored to have been selected by the president, and the award encouraged Andy during a difficult time. He expressed sincere appreciation for the medal. In a letter to Robert F. Kennedy, the former president's brother, Andy said that receiving the Presidential Medal of Freedom was "the most gratifying thing that ever happened to me."

Edward Frascino illustrated The Trumpet of the Swan. *Here Louis the swan plays taps over Camp Kookooskoos.*

THIRTEEN

Louis and Serena

1968–1975

Throughout their marriage, Andy and Katharine had enjoyed a comfortable standard of living, adequately supported by their positions at *The New Yorker* and by book sales. But after the Whites' semi-retirement from the magazine in 1957, their finances were quickly consumed by doctors' bills, hospital expenses, the salaries of home nursing attendants, and farm help.

Andy worried about money. Despite the success of *Charlotte's Web,* his contract only allowed him to collect a small amount of his royalties each year.

Inspired by the need to earn money, Andy decided it was time to write another children's book. He had an idea for a story about a trumpeter swan who is unable to speak.

In 1968 Andy once again teamed up with Howard "Cush" Cushman, who was living in Pennsylvania. The two men had corresponded with each other over the years since their cross-country adventure. Andy now asked Cush for help in researching trumpeter swans on Bird Lake at the Zoological Gardens in Pennsylvania. He wanted to know how the swans looked, how they smelled, and what they sounded like.

Cush sent Andy the information he needed, along with photographs of the swans. Andy also drew upon his knowledge of loons to describe the swans' behavior. He remembered a scene from almost 30 years earlier at Camp Otter, when he and James Thurber had set a camera on a tripod in the back of a canoe and paddled across the lake to take pictures of a loon's nest. The mother loon had flown frantically around the canoe in an effort to distract them from her day-old chick and an unhatched egg. Andy had photographed the chick as it took its first flight off the nest to join its mother on the lake. Andy's story incorporated other scenes from his past, such as a ranch he had briefly worked at in Montana. By Christmas Andy had completed two-thirds of the book. "I am 69 years old," he noted. "It's the last third that I wonder about."

It took 11 more months to finish *The Trumpet of the Swan*. Andy described the writing process as "hard work" and "often a pure headache." He spent several hours every morning, frequently in his boathouse, writing and rewriting.

During that time, Katharine was hospitalized for 13 weeks because of a spinal fracture and other health problems. Back at the farm, she required a hospital-type bed and more nursing attention.

On July 11, 1969, Andy turned 70 years old. A writer for the *New York Times* drove out to the farm to interview him. The *Times* article resulted in another flood of fan mail and more visitors.

That fall Andy submitted the book to his publisher. He worried that he had not put sufficient time into rewriting the text, but he was eager to get it published.

Generally, an author has no choice in who will illustrate

a book, so Andy deferred to Ursula Nordstrom, his editor, for her choice of an illustrator. Although pleased with the drawings Garth Williams had made for *Stuart Little* and *Charlotte's Web*, Andy said that he did not feel obligated to use Williams for the new book.

As it turned out, Williams was in Mexico, and Andy was anxious for a spring release of the book. Harper & Row, the successor to Harper and Brothers, decided to use drawings by Edward Frascino.

Williams felt hurt by this decision. Andy wrote to him: "I am very sad tonight...I have always felt immensely in your debt...I am unhappy about being separated from you after these many fine and rewarding years. I never expected it to happen, and I never wanted it to happen."

For the cover of his new book, Andy envisioned a drawing of the baby swan Louis pulling on Sam's shoelace while a protective parent swan lingers in the background. Andy asked a local artist to paint the scene. Frascino used this painting to draw the cover.

The Trumpet of the Swan appeared in bookstores in the spring of 1970. It is about Louis, a trumpeter swan who is unable to say "Ko hoh" like his brothers and sisters. Louis's parents fear their son will have difficulty attracting a mate when he is fully grown.

With the help of a young boy named Sam Beaver, Louis goes to school and learns to read and write. He carries a slate around his neck and uses chalk to write words. Unfortunately, the other swans cannot read. Louis falls in love with Serena, but she pays little attention to the swan who cannot court her with the traditional calls of "Ko-hoh."

Louis's father thinks that his son could communicate with a trumpet. He flies to a music store in Billings, Montana,

All day, Louis tries to make a noise on his new trumpet.

crashes through the window, and steals a beautiful trumpet with a red cord.

After much difficulty, Louis learns to play the trumpet. To earn money to repay the music-store owner, Louis works as a camp bugler, serenades passengers on the Swan Boat in Boston, and performs in a Philadelphia night club. He also gives free concerts on a lake in the Philadelphia Zoo.

One night during a terrible storm, Serena is caught by the wind and lands on the lake. After she recovers, Louis woos her with his beautiful trumpet music. In the end, the two swans are happily in love, and Louis is able to repay the music-store owner.

As Andy had hoped, *The Trumpet of the Swan* was a success. The book reached the top of the *New York Times* list of best-selling children's books, temporarily edging out *Charlotte's Web*, which was still a favorite. In 1972 Andy condensed *The Trumpet of the Swan* to four pages of text, and the Philadelphia Orchestra set it to music for a symphony performance.

Andy received many honors, including the Laura Ingalls Wilder award, a National Medal for Literature, and another medal from the American Academy of Arts and Letters. He especially cherished awards and certificates given to him by children.

Andy found more ways to earn money. For years he had resisted attempts to make *Charlotte's Web* into a movie. But in 1973, he consented to Hanna-Barbera's animated film version, despite his opinion that the film contained too many inappropriate songs and that his own suggestions were ignored. Katharine felt responsible for Andy's unhappiness with the film. She knew that he was making sacrifices in order to care for her.

In the fall of 1975, Katharine suffered congestive heart failure. While she recovered in the local hospital, Andy wrote to her: "This made me realize more than anything else ever has how much I love you and how little life would mean to me were you not here."

Andy at home with his dog Susy

❧ FOURTEEN ❧

E. B. White

1976–1985

With *The Trumpet of the Swan* completed, Andy focused on several other moneymaking projects. One was a collection of the letters he had written over the years. Relatives, friends, and acquaintances searched their attics and found many of the letters Andy had penned as a boy, during his trip west, as a young writer in New York, and as a famous author living in Maine. *The Letters of E. B. White*, edited by Dorothy Lobrano Guth, appeared in 1976. The book offers a unique glimpse into the life of a very private man. The letters reveal not only his wit and his friendships, but also his constant worries about his health and his dislike for public attention.

The success of his books lessened Andy's concern about finances. But Katharine's health declined steadily. Her eyesight dimmed, and she frequently required emergency doses of oxygen.

On July 20, 1977, Katharine again suffered congestive heart failure. The fire department brought oxygen in response to the Whites' call for help. This time, though, the attack was more serious, and an ambulance rushed Katharine to the hospital.

Her fever flared and the medication was useless. Katharine could not talk.

Pensively watching a heart monitor, Andy stayed in the intensive care unit with his wife. At five o'clock in the afternoon, Katharine died. Andy wrote, "She seemed beautiful to me the first time I saw her, and she seemed beautiful when I gave her the small kiss that was goodbye."

Carrying out Katharine's request, the family held only a simple graveside service for her. For his own private reasons, Andy chose not to attend, although he wrote the program for the service, which included a poem he had written for his wife 40 years earlier. He later planted an oak tree by her grave.

Andy countered his loneliness with more literary projects. In the years after Katharine's death, he revised *The Elements of Style*, produced *The Essays of E. B. White*, and compiled *Poems and Sketches of E. B. White*. He also wrote an introduction for a book Katharine had left unfinished, a collection of her garden essays entitled *Onward and Upward in the Garden*.

In 1979 Andy finally succeeded in withdrawing the balance of the royalties due to him for *Charlotte's Web*. The payment was large, over half a million dollars, and a significant portion went to the government for taxes.

By the time he was 83 years old, arthritis made it difficult for Andy to type and perform simple tasks such as tying his shoes. A degenerated retina claimed the vision in his right eye. His hearing worsened, and he suffered from a heart blockage.

Still, Andy enjoyed nature. His love for the natural world, especially the farm, never waned. Although lonely in his big 11-room house, he would not consider moving away.

And the Belgrade Lakes still beckoned. Andy bought himself a new canoe, much like the one his father had given

E. B. White's drawing of his beloved farm in Maine

him as an 11-year-old. He enjoyed being on the water, swimming, and camping by Great Pond.

In his final years, several small strokes interfered with his ability to speak. Joel lived nearby, and he stopped to visit twice a day. He often read to his father from Andy's own works.

On October 1, 1985, Andy died of Alzheimer's disease. He was at home in Maine at the time. Like his wife, Andy had requested that his body be cremated and that there be no funeral service.

Andy White looks out over the ocean in Maine.

EPILOGUE

A memorial service for E. B. White was held at the Congregational Church in Blue Hill on October 26, 1985. Three hundred people attended, sitting on wooden benches as the sun shone through stained-glass windows. The printed folder that accompanied the service featured a picture of Andy as a grown man, swinging on the barn rope. A small flower, the "wild flag," decorated the cover. Inside appeared Andy's love poem to Katharine, "Natural History."

Roger Angell, who had since become a writer for *The New Yorker*, spoke of the advice his stepfather gave him in finding his own style. Friends and family members shared kind words for the quiet man who had touched them all.

Andy's ashes are buried next to Katharine's in Brooklin Cemetery at Brooklin, Maine. His words, however, continue to bring joy to children and adults. *Stuart Little* was adapted for a television series in 1966, narrated by Johnny Carson. Today, sales of the book have reached over three million copies.

In 1990 a new collection of Andy's essays and editorials were published in the book *Writings from the New Yorker*

1927–1976. Readers still turn to Andy's essays for encouragement and advice on environmental and social issues.

The popularity of *Charlotte's Web* remains steady. Over six million copies of the book have been sold. The story can be read in over 20 languages and heard on a cassette recording. For the last several years, it has been on the *Publishers Weekly* list of all-time best-selling children's paperback books.

Although a very shy and private man, Andy shared his life with both children and adults through his essays, letters, and stories. To his readers, he is both "a true friend and a good writer."

Sources

12 E. B. White, *One Man's Meat* (New York: Harper & Brothers, 1944), 8.

12 Ibid.

12 *Letters of E. B. White*, ed. Dorothy Lobrano Guth (New York: Harper & Row, 1976), 281.

12 Letter, 21 October 1908, E. B. White Collection, Cornell University Library. Courtesy of the Division of Rare and Manuscript Collections, Cornell University Library.

22 *Letters of E. B. White*, 10.

22–23 E. B. White, "Pink Hats," *The Mount Vernon High School Oracle*, March 1916.

23 E. B. White, Editorial, *The Mount Vernon High School Oracle*, January-February 1917.

23 E. B. White, Editorial, *The Mount Vernon High School Oracle*, May-June 1917.

23 White, *One Man's Meat*, 110.

26 Scott Elledge, *E. B. White: A Biography* (New York: Norton, 1984), 52.

28 William Strunk, Jr., and E. B. White, *The Elements of Style*, 3rd ed. (New York: Macmillan, 1979), xiii.

29 White, *One Man's Meat*, 114.

29 E. B. White, "Free Speech and Bad Judgment," *Cornell Daily Sun*, 10 December 1920.

36–37 *Letters of E. B. White*, 38–39.

38 Ibid., 47.

40 E. B. White, *The Second Tree from the Corner* (New York: Harper & Brothers, 1954), 11.

40 Ibid., 12.

42 *Essays of E. B. White* (New York: Harper & Row, 1977), 179.

43 *Letters of E. B. White*, 69.

48 E. B. White, "Child's Play," *The New Yorker*, 26 December 1925, 17.

48 *Letters of E. B. White*, 324.

48 Elledge, *E. B. White*, 109.

49 E. B. White, *Ho Hum* (New York: Farrar & Rinehart, 1931), 18.

49 Ibid., 98.

50 White, *The Second Tree from the Corner*, 12.

57 Elledge, *E. B. White*, 170.

57 *Letters of E. B. White*, 89.

58 Ibid., 91.

62 Ralph Ingersoll, "The New Yorker," *Fortune*, August 1934, 86.

62 Ibid., 97.

63 *Letters of E. B. White*, 118.

65 Ibid., 125.

67 Ibid., 130.

67 Ibid.

68 Ibid., 131–132.

69 Ibid., 155.

69 Ibid., 154.

69 Ibid., 156.

72 Ibid., 169.

75 White, *One Man's Meat*, 127.

76 Ibid., 25.

77 *Letters of E. B. White*, 194.

85 E. B. White, *Stuart Little* (New York: Harper & Row, 1973,) 131.

85 *Letters of E. B. White*, 406.

85 Ibid., 478.

85 White, *Stuart Little*, 131.

87 *Letters of E. B. White*, 280.

88 Ibid., 285.

88 Ibid., 286.

88 Ibid., 285.

90   *E. B. White: Writings from
      The New Yorker 1927–1976,* ed.
      Rebecca Dale (New York:
      HarperCollins, 1990), 233.

93   *Letters of E. B. White,* 314.

93   Ibid., 331.

94–95 Folder A, E. B. White
      Collection, Cornell University
      Library. Courtesy of the
      Division of Rare and
      Manuscript Collections, Cornell
      University Library.

95   Ibid.

98   Ursula Nordstrom, "Stuart,
      Wilbur, Charlotte: A Tale of
      Tales," *New York Times Book
      Review,* 12 May 1974. Copyright
      © 1974 by the New York
      Times Company. Reprinted by
      permission.

99   E. B. White, *Charlotte's Web*
      (New York: Harper & Row,
      1980), 31.

99   Ibid., 50.

99   Ibid., 140.

100   Ibid., 144.

100   Ibid., 184.

103   *Letters of E. B. White,* 373.

103   Ibid., 415.

104   Ibid., 391.

105–106 Ibid., 470.

108   Program accompanying
      Presidential Medal, E. B.
      White Collection, Cornell
      University Library. Courtesy
      of the Division of Rare and
      Manuscript Collections,
      Cornell University Library.

109   *Letters of E. B. White,* 513.

112   Ibid., 573.

112   Ibid., 582.

113   Ibid., 592.

115   Ibid., 657.

118   Elledge, *E. B. White,* 354.

122   White, *Charlotte's Web,* 184.

Bibliography

Writings of E. B. White, in chronological order

Ho Hum: Newsbreaks from "The New Yorker." New York: Farrar & Rinehart, 1931.

Every Day Is Saturday. New York: Harper & Brothers, 1934.

Quo Vadimus? Or the Case for the Bicycle. New York: Harper & Brothers, 1939.

One Man's Meat. New York: Harper & Brothers, 1942.

Stuart Little. New York: Harper & Brothers, 1945.

The Wild Flag. Boston: Houghton Mifflin, 1946.

Here Is New York. New York: Harper & Brothers, 1949.

Charlotte's Web. New York: Harper & Brothers, 1952.

The Second Tree from the Corner. New York: Harper & Brothers, 1954.

The Elements of Style. By William Strunk, Jr. With revisions, an introduction, and a new chapter on writing by E. B. White. New York: Macmillan, 1959.

The Points of My Compass: Letters from the East, the West, the North, and the South. New York: Harper & Row, 1962.

An E. B. White Reader. Edited by William W. Watt and Robert W. Bradford. New York: Harper & Row, 1966.

The Trumpet of the Swan. New York: Harper & Row, 1970.

Letters of E. B. White. Edited by Dorothy Lobrano Guth. New York: Harper & Row, 1970.

Essays of E. B. White. New York: Harper & Row, 1977.

Poems and Sketches of E. B. White. New York: Harper & Row, 1981.

E. B. White: Writings from The New Yorker 1927–1976. Edited by Rebecca Dale. New York: HarperCollins, 1990.

E. B. White Collection, Cornell University, Rare and Manuscript Collections, University Library, Ithaca, New York.

Other Sources

Davis, Linda H. *Onward and Upward: A Biography of Katharine S. White.* New York: Harper & Row, 1987.

Elledge, Scott. *E. B. White: A Biography.* New York: Norton, 1984.

Gill, Brendan. *Here at The New Yorker.* New York: Random House, 1975.

Hall, Katherine Romans, comp. *E. B. White: A Bibliographic Catalogue of Printed Materials in the Department of Rare Books, Cornell University Library.* New York: Garland, 1979.

Kramer, Dale. *Ross and The New Yorker.* New York: Doubleday, 1951.

Index

127

Photo Acknowledgments

The photographs have been reproduced by permission of: pp. 1, 2, 6, 8, 10, 11, 13, 14, 16, 17, 18, 20, 21, 24, 26, 28, 31, 41, 44, 54, 60, 61, 62, 64, 66, 89, 91 (top), 94, 95, 96, 97, 119, Division of Rare and Manuscript Collections, Cornell University Library; pp. 9, 30, 32, 35, 37, 39, 70, 72, 74, 75, 79, 82, 86, 91 (bottom), 102, 106, 107, 109, Joel and Allene White; p. 46, Archive Photos; p. 51, Cover by E. B. White © 1932, 1960 The New Yorker Magazine, Inc. All Rights Reserved; p. 53, The Bettman Archive; pp. 59, 107, Nancy Stableford; pp. 80, 84, 92, 98, 101, 110, 114, Reprinted by permission of HarperCollins Publishers; pp. 116, 120, Jim Kalett.

Front cover photograph courtesy of the Division of Rare and Manuscript Collections, Cornell University Library. Back cover illustration by Garth Williams, reproduced by permission of HarperCollins.